Mr. Dooley's Philosophy

By

Finley Peter Dunne

Mr. Dooley's Philosophy

A BOOK REVIEW

"Well sir," said Mr. Dooley, "I jus' got hold iv a book, Hinnissy, that suits me up to th' handle, a gran' book, th' grandest iver seen. Ye know I'm not much throubled be lithrachoor, havin' manny worries iv me own, but I'm not prejudiced again' books. I am not. Whin a rale good book comes along I'm as quick as anny wan to say it isn't so bad, an' this here book is fine. I tell ye 'tis fine."

"What is it?" Mr. Hennessy asked languidly.

"'Tis 'Th' Biography iv a Hero be Wan who Knows.' 'Tis 'Th' Darin' Exploits iv a Brave Man be an Actual Eye Witness.' 'Tis 'Th' Account iv th' Desthruction iv Spanish Power in th' Ant Hills,' as it fell fr'm th' lips iv Tiddy Rosenfelt an' was took down be his own hands. Ye see 'twas this way, Hinnissy, as I r-read th' book. Whin Tiddy was blowed up in th' harbor iv Havana he instantly concluded they must be war. He debated th' question long an' earnestly an' fin'lly passed a jint resolution declarin' war. So far so good. But there was no wan to carry it on. What shud he do? I will lave th' janial author tell th' story in his own wurruds.

"'Th' sicrety iv war had offered me,' he says, 'th' command of a rig'mint,' he says, 'but I cud not consint to remain in Tampa while perhaps less audacious heroes was at th' front,' he says. 'Besides,' he says, 'I felt I was incompetent f'r to command a rig'mint raised be another,' he says. 'I detarmined to raise wan iv me own,' he says. 'I selected fr'm me acquaintances in th' West,' he says, 'men that had thravelled with me acrost th' desert an' th' storm-wreathed mountain,' he says, 'sharin' me burdens an' at times confrontin' perils almost as gr-reat as anny that beset me path,' he says. 'Together we had faced th' turrors iv th' large but vilent West,' he says, 'an' these brave men had seen me with me trusty rifle shootin' down th' buffalo, th' elk, th' moose, th' grizzly bear, th' mountain goat,' he says, 'th' silver man, an' other ferocious beasts iv thim parts,' he says. 'An' they niver flinched,' he says. 'In a few days I had thim perfectly tamed,' he says, 'an' ready to go annywhere I led,' he says. 'On th' thransport goi'n to Cubia,' he says, 'I wud stand beside wan iv these r-rough men threatin' him as a akel, which he was in ivrything but birth, education, rank an' courage, an' together we wud look up at th' admirable stars iv that tolerable southern sky an' quote th' bible fr'm Walt Whitman,' he says. 'Honest, loyal, thrue-hearted la-ads, how kind I was to thim,' he says."

{Illustration: Read the articles by Roosevelt and Davis in the Car Fare Magazine}

"'We had no sooner landed in Cubia than it become nicessry f'r me to take command iv th' ar-rmy which I did at wanst. A number of days was spint be me in reconnoitring, attinded on'y be me brave an' fluent body guard, Richard Harding Davis. I discovered that th' inimy was heavily inthrenched on th' top iv San Juon hill immejiately in front iv me. At this time it become apparent that I was handicapped be th' prisence iv th' ar-rmy,' he says. 'Wan day whin I was about to charge a block house sturdily definded be an ar-rmy corps undher Gin'ral Tamale, th' brave Castile that I afthwards killed with a small ink-eraser that I always carry, I r-ran into th' entire military force iv th' United States lying on its stomach. 'If ye won't fight,' says I, 'let me go through, 'I says. 'Who ar-re ye?' says they. 'Colonel Rosenfelt,' says I. 'Oh, excuse me,' says the gin'ral in command (if me mimry serves me thrue it was Miles) r-risin' to his knees an' salutin'. This showed me 'twud be impossible f'r to carry th' war to a successful con-clusion unless I was free, so I sint th' ar-rmy home an' attackted San Juon hill. Ar-rmed on'y with a small thirty-two which I used in th' West to shoot th' fleet prairie dog, I climbed that precipitous ascent in th' face iv th' most gallin' fire I iver knew or heerd iv. But I had a few r-rounds iv gall mesilf an' what cared I? I dashed madly on cheerin' as I wint. Th' Spanish throops was dhrawn up in a long line in th' formation known among military men as a long line. I fired at th' man nearest to me an' I knew be th' expression iv his face that th' trusty bullet wint home. It passed through his frame, he fell, an' wan little home in far-off Catalonia was made happy be th' thought that their riprisintative had been kilt be th' future governor iv New York. Th' bullet sped on its mad flight an' passed through th' intire line fin'lly imbeddin' itself in th' abdomen iv th' Ar-rch-bishop iv Santiago eight miles away. This ended th' war.'

"'They has been some discussion as to who was th' first man to r-reach th' summit iv San Juon hill. I will not attempt to dispute th' merits iv th' manny gallant sojers, statesmen, corryspondints an' kinetoscope men who claim th' distinction. They ar-re all brave men an' if they wish to wear my laurels they may. I have so manny annyhow that it keeps me broke havin' thim blocked an' irned. But I will say f'r th' binifit iv Posterity that I was th' on'y man I see. An I had a tillyscope.'"

"I have thried, Hinnissy," Mr. Dooley continued, "to give you a fair idee iv th' contints iv this remarkable book, but what I've tol' ye is on'y what Hogan calls an outline iv th' principal pints. Ye'll have to r-read th' book ye'ersilf to get a thrue conciption. I haven't time f'r to tell ye th' wurruk Tiddy did in ar-rmin' an' equippin' himself, how he fed himsilf, how he steadied himsilf in battle an' encouraged himsilf with a few well-chosen wurruds whin th' sky was darkest. Ye'll have to take a squint into th' book ye'ersilf to l'arn thim things."

"I won't do it," said Mr. Hennessy. "I think Tiddy Rosenfelt is all r-right an' if he wants to blow his hor-rn lave him do it."

"Thrue f'r ye," said Mr. Dooley, "an' if his valliant deeds didn't get into this book 'twud be a long time befure they appeared in Shafter's histhry iv th' war. No man that bears a gredge again' himsilf 'll iver be governor iv a state. An' if Tiddy done it all he ought to say so an' relieve th' suspinse. But if I was him I'd call th' book 'Alone in Cubia.'"

AMERICANS ABROAD

"I wondher," said Mr. Dooley, "what me Dutch frind Oom Paul'll think whin he hears that Willum Waldorf Asthor has given four thousan' pounds or twinty thousan' iv our money as a conthribution to th' British governmint?"

"Who's Willum Waldorf Asthor?" Mr. Hennessy asked. "I niver heerd iv him."

"Ye wudden't," said Mr. Dooley. "He don't thravel in ye'er set. Willum Waldorf Asthor is a gintleman that wanst committed th' sin iv bein' bor-rn in this counthry. Ye know what orig-inal sin is, Hinnissy. Ye was bor-rn with wan an' I was bor-rn with wan an' ivrybody was bor-rn with wan. 'Twas took out iv me be Father Tuomy with holy wather first an' be me father aftherward with a sthrap. But I niver cud find out what it was. Th' sins I've committed since, I'm sure iv. They're painted red an' carry a bell an' whin I'm awake in bed they stan' out on th' wall like th' ilicthric signs they have down be State sthreet in front iv th' clothin' stores. But I'll go to th' grave without knowin' exactly what th' black orig-inal sin was I committed. All I know is I done wrong. But with Willum Waldorf Asthor 'tis dif'rent. I say 'tis diff'rent with Willum Waldorf Asthor. His orig-inal sin was bein' bor-rn in New York. He cudden't do anything about it. Nawthin' in this counthry wud wipe it out. He built a hotel intinded f'r jooks who had no sins but thim iv their own makin', but even th' sight iv their haughty bills cud not efface th' stain. He thried to live down his crime without success an' he thried to live down to it be runnin' f'r congress, but it was no go. No matther where he wint among his counthrymen in England some wan wud find out he was bor-rn in New York an' th' man that ownded th' house where he was spindin' th' night wud ast him if he was a cannibal an' had he anny Indyan blood in his veins. 'Twas like seein' a fine lookin' man with an intellecjal forehead an' handsome, dar-rk brown eyes an' admirin' him, an' thin larnin' his name is Mudd J. Higgins. His accint was proper an' his clothes didn't fit him right, but he was not bor-rn in th' home iv his dayscindants, an' whin he walked th' sthreets iv London he knew ivry polisman was sayin': 'There goes a man that pretinds to be happy, but a dark sorrow is gnawin' at his bosom. He looks as if he was at home, but he was bor-rn in New York, Gawd help him.'"

{Illustration}

"So this poor way-worn sowl, afther thryin' ivry other rimidy fr'm dhrivin' a coach to failin' to vote, at las' sought out th' rile high clark iv th' coort an' says he: 'Behold,' he says, 'an onhappy man,' he says. 'With millyons in me pocket, two hotels an' onlimited credit, 'he says, 'me hear-rt is gray,' he says. 'Poor sowl,' says th' clark iv th' coort, 'What's ailin' ye'?' he says. 'Have ye committed some gr-reat crime?' he says. 'Partly,' says Willum Waldorf Asthor. 'It was partly me an' partly me folks,' he says. 'I was,' he says, in a voice broken be tears, 'I was,' he says, 'bor-rn in New York,' he says. Th' clark made th' sign iv th' cross an' says he: 'Ye shudden't have come here,' he says. 'Poor afflicted wretch,' he says, 'ye need a clargyman,' he says. 'Why did ye seek me out?' he says. 'Because,' says Willum Waldorf Asthor, 'I wish,' he says, 'fr to renounce me sinful life,' he says. 'I wish to be bor-rn anew,' he says. An' th' clark bein' a kind man helps him out. An' Willum Waldorf Asthor renounced fealty to all foreign sovereigns, princes an' potentates an' especially Mack th' Wanst, or Twict, iv th' United States an' Sulu an' all his wur-ruks an' he come out iv th' coort with his hat cocked over his eye, with a step jaunty and high, afther years iv servile freedom a bondman at last!

"So he's a citizen iv Gr-reat Britain now an' a lile subject iv th' Queen like you was Hinnissy befure ye was r-run out."

"I niver was," said Mr. Hennessy. "Sure th' Queen iv England was renounced f'r me long befure I did it f'r mesilf—to vote."

"Well, niver mind," Mr. Dooley continued, "he's a citizen iv England an' he has a castle that's as big as a hotel, on'y nobody goes there excipt thim that's ast, an' not all of those, an' he owns a newspaper an' th' editor iv it's the Prince iv Wales an' th' rayporthers is all jooks an' th' Archbishop iv Canterbury r-runs th' ilivator, an' slug wan in th' printin' office is th' Impror iv Germany in disgeese. 'Tis a pa-per I'd like to see. I'd like to know how th' Jook iv Marlbro'd do th' McGovern fight. An' some day Willum Waldorf Asthor'll be able to wurruk f'r his own pa-aper, f'r he's goin' to be a earl or a markess or a jook or somethin' gran'. Ye can't be anny iv these things without money, Hinnissy, an' he has slathers iv it."

"Where does he get it?" demanded Mr. Hennessy.

"F'rm this counthry," said Mr. Dooley.

"I shud think," Mr. Hennessy protested stoutly, "if he's ashamed iv this counthry he wudden't want to take money f'rm it."

"That's where ye're wrong," Mr. Dooley replied. "Take money annywhere ye find it. I'd take money f'rm England, much as I despise that formerly haughty but now dejected land, if I cud get anny from there. An' whin ye come down to it, I dinnaw as I blame Willum Waldorf Asthor f'r shiftin' his allegiance. Ivry wan to his taste as th' man said whin he dhrank out iv th' fire extinguisher. It depinds on how ye feel. If ye ar-re a tired la-ad an' wan without much fight in ye, livin' in this counthry is like thryin' to read th' Lives iv the Saints at a meetin' iv th' Clan-na-Gael. They'se no quiet f'r annybody. They's a fight on ivry minyit iv th' time. Ye may say to ye'ersilf: 'I'll lave these la-ads roll each other as much as they plaze, but I'll set here in th' shade an' dhrink me milk punch, but ye can't do it. Some wan 'll say, 'Look at that gazabo settin' out there alone. He's too proud f'r to jine in our simple dimmycratic festivities. Lave us go over an' bate him on th' eye.' An' they do it. Now if ye have fightin' blood in ye'er veins ye hastily gulp down yeer dhrink an' hand ye'er assailant wan that does him no kind iv good, an' th' first thing ye know ye're in th thick iv it an' its scrap, scrap, scrap till th' undhertaker calls f'r to measure ye. An' 'tis tin to wan they'se somethin' doin' at th' fun'ral that ye're sorry ye missed. That's life in America. Tis a gloryous big fight, a rough an' tumble fight, a Donnybrook fair three thousan' miles wide an' a ruction in ivry block. Head an' ban's an' feet an' th' pitchers on th' wall. No holds barred. Fight fair but don't f'rget th' other la-ad may not know where th' belt line is. No polisman in sight. A man's down with twenty on top iv him wan minyit. Th' next he's settin' on th' pile usin' a base-ball bat on th' neighbor next below him. 'Come on, boys, f'r 'tis growin' late, an' no wan's been kilt yet. Glory be, but this is th' life!'

"Now, if I'm tired I don't want to fight. A man bats me in th' eye an' I call f'r th' polis. They isn't a polisman in sight. I say to th' man that poked me: 'Sir, I fain wud sleep.' 'Get up,' he says, 'an' be doin',' he says. 'Life is rale, life is earnest,' he says, 'an' man was made to fight,' he says, fetchin' me a kick. An' if I'm tired I say, 'What's th' use? I've got plenty iv money in me inside pocket. I'll go to a place where they don't know how to fight. I'll go where I can get something but an argymint f'r me money an' where I won't have to rassle with th' man that bates me carpets, ayether,' I says, 'f'r fifty cints overcharge or good govermint,' I says. An' I pike off to what Hogan calls th' effete monarchies iv Europe an' no wan walks on me toes, an' ivry man I give a dollar to becomes an acrobat an' I live comfortably an' die a markess! Th' divvle I do!

"That's what I was goin' to say," Mr. Hennessy remarked. "Ye wudden't live annywhere but here."

"No," said Mr. Dooley, "I wudden't. I'd rather be Dooley iv Chicago than th' Earl iv Peltvule. It must be that I'm iv th' fightin' kind."

SERVANT GIRL PROBLEM

Whin Congress gets through expellin' mimbers that believes so much in mathrimony that they carry it into ivry relation iv life an' opens th' dure iv Chiny so that an American can go in there as free as a Chinnyman can come into this refuge iv th' opprissed iv th' wurruld, I hope'twill turn its attintion to th' gr-reat question now confrontin' th' nation—th' question iv what we shall do with our hired help. What shall we do with thim?

"We haven't anny," said Mr. Hennessy.

"No," said Mr. Dooley. "Ar-rchey r-road has no servant girl problem. Th' rule is ivry woman her own cook an' ivry man his own futman, an' be th' same token we have no poly-gamy problem an' no open dure problem an' no Ph'lippeen problem. Th' on'y problem in Ar-rchey r-road is how manny times does round steak go into twelve at wan dollar-an-a-half a day. But east iv th' r-red bridge, Hinnissy, wan iv th' most cryin' issues iv th' hour is: What shall we do with our hired help? An' if Congress don't take hold iv it we ar-re a rooned people."

"'Tis an ol' problem an' I've seen it arise an' shake its gory head ivry few years whiniver th' Swede popylation got wurruk an' begun bein' marrid, thus rayjoocin' th' visible supply iv help. But it seems 'tis deeper thin that. I see be letters in th' pa-apers that servants is insolent, an' that they won't go to wurruk onless they like th' looks iv their employers, an' that they rayfuse to live in th' counthry. Why anny servant shud rayfuse to live in th' counthry is more thin I can see. Ye'd think that this disreputable class'd give annything to lave th' crowded tinimints iv a large city where they have frinds be th' hundherds an' know th' polisman on th' bate an' can go out to hateful dances an' moonlight picnics—ye'd think these unforchnate slaves'd be delighted to live in Mulligan's subdivision, amid th' threes an' flowers an' bur-rds. Gettin' up at four o'clock in th' mornin' th' singin' iv th' full-throated alarm clock is answered be an invisible choir iv songsters, as Shakespere says, an' ye see th' sun rise over th' hills as ye go out to carry in a ton iv coal. All day long ye meet no wan as ye thrip over th' coal-scuttle, happy in ye'er tile an' ye'er heart is enlivened be th' thought that th' childher in th' front iv th' house ar-re growin' sthrong on th' fr-resh counthry air. Besides they'se always cookin' to do. At night ye can set be th' fire an' improve ye'er mind be r-readin' half th' love story in th' part iv th' pa-aper that th' cheese come home in, an' whin ye're through with that, all ye have to do is to climb a ladder to th' roof an' fall through th' skylight an' ye're in bed."

"But wud ye believe it, Hinnissy, manny iv these misguided women rayfuse f'r to take a job that aint in a city. They prefer th' bustle an' roar iv th' busy marts iv thrade, th' sthreet car, th' saloon on three corners an' th' church on wan, th' pa-apers ivry mornin' with pitchers iv th' s'ciety fav'rite that's just thrown up a good job at Armours to elope with th' well-known club man who used to be yard-masther iv th' three B's, G, L, & N., th' shy peek into th' dhry-goods store, an' other base luxuries, to a free an' healthy life in th' counthry between iliven P.M. an' four A.M. Wensdahs an' Sundahs. 'Tis worse thin that, Hinnissy, f'r whin they ar-re in th' city they seem to dislike their wurruk an' manny iv thim ar-re givin' up splindid jobs with good large families where they have no chanst to spind their salaries, if they dhraw thim, an' takin' places in shops, an' gettin' marrid an' adoptin' other devices that will give thim th' chanst f'r to wear out their good clothes. 'Tis a horrible situation. Riley th' conthractor dhropped in here th' other day in his horse an' buggy on his way to the dhrainage canal an' he was all wurruked up over th' question. 'Why,' he says, ''tis scand'lous th' way servants act,' he says. 'Mrs. Riley has hystrics,' he says. 'An' ivry two or three nights whin I come home,' he says, 'I have to win a fight again' a cook with a stove lid befure I can move me family off th' fr-ront stoop,' he says. 'We threat thim well too,' he says. 'I gave th' las' wan we had fifty cints an' a cook book at Chris'mas an' th' next day she left befure breakfast,' he says. 'What naytionalties do ye hire?' says I. 'I've thried thim all,' he says, 'an',' he says, 'I'll say this in shame,' he says, 'that th' Irish ar-re th' worst,' he says. 'Well,' says I, 'ye need have no shame,' I says, 'f'r'tis on'y th' people that ar-re good servants that'll niver be masthers,' I says. 'Th' Irish ar-re no good as servants because they ar-re too good,' I says. 'Th' Dutch ar-re no good because they aint good enough. No matther how they start they get th' noodle habit. I had wan, wanst, an' she got so she put noodles in me tay,' I says. 'Th' Swedes ar-re all right but they always get marrid th' sicond day. Ye'll have a polisman at th' dure with a warrant f'r th' arrist iv ye'er cook if ye hire a Boheemyan,' I says. 'Coons'd be all right but they're liable f'r to hand ye ye'er food in ragtime, an' if ye ordher pork-chops f'r dinner an' th' hall is long,'tis little ye'll have to eat whin th' platter's set down,' I says. 'No,' says I, 'they'se no naytionality now livin' in this counthry that're nathral bor-rn servants,' I says. 'If ye want to save throuble,' I says, 'ye'll import ye'er help. They'se a race iv people livin' in Cinthral Africa that'd be jus' r-right. They niver sleep, tkey can carry twice their weight on their backs, they have no frinds, they wear no clothes, they can't read, they can't dance an' they don't dhrink. Th' fact is they're thoroughly oneddycated. If ye cud tache thim to cook an' take care iv childher they'd be th' best servants,' says I. 'An' what d'ye call thim?' says he. 'I f'rget,' says I. An' he wint away mad."

"Sure an' he's a nice man to be talkin' iv servants," said Mr. Hennessy. "He was a gintleman's man in th' ol' counthry an' I used to know his wife whin she wurruked f'r ——"

"S-sh," said Mr. Dooley. "They're beyond that now. Besides they speak fr'm experyence. An' mebbe that's th' throuble. We're always harder with our own kind thin with others. 'Tis I that'd be th' fine cinsor iv a bartinder's wurruk. Th' more ye ought to be a servant ye'ersilf th' more difficult'tis f'r ye to get along with servants. I can holler to anny man fr'm th' top iv a buildin' an' make him tur-rn r-round, but if I come down to th' sthreet where he can see I aint anny bigger thin he is, an' holler at him, 'tis twenty to wan if he tur-rns r-round he'll hit me in th' eye. We have a servant girl problem because, Hinnissy, it isn't manny years since we first begun to have servant girls. But I hope Congress'll take it up. A smart Congress like th' wan we have now ought to be able to spare a little time fr'm its preparation iv new Jims iv speech f'r th' third reader an' rig up a bill that'd make keepin' house a recreation while so softenin' th' spirit iv th' haughty sign iv a noble race in th' kitchen that cookin' buckwheat cakes on a hot day with th' aid iv a bottle iv smokeless powdher'd not cause her f'r to sind a worthy man to his office in slippers an' without a hat."

"Ah," said Mr. Hennessy, the simple democrat. "It wud be all r-right if women'd do their own cookin'."

"Well," said Mr. Dooley. "'Twud be a return to Jacksonyan simplicity, an' 'twud be a gr-reat thing f'r th' resthrant business."

THE TRANSVAAL

"It looks like war," said Mr. Hennessy, who had been glancing at the flaming head-lines of an evening paper over Mr. Dooley's shoulder.

"It always does," said Mr. Dooley. "Since th' Czar iv Rooshia inthrajooced his no-fight risolution, they'se been no chanst that they wudden't be ructious."

"An' what's it all about?" demanded Mr. Hennessy. "I can't make head nor tail iv it at all, at all."

"Well ye see 'tis this way," said Mr. Dooley. "Ye see th' Boers is a simple, pasthral people that goes about their business in their own way, raisin' hell with ivrybody. They was bor-rn with an aversion to society an' whin th' English come they lit out befure thim, not likin' their looks. Th' English kept comin' an' the Boers kept movin' till they cudden't move anny further without bumpin' into th' Soodanese ar-rmy an' thin they settled down an' says they, 'This far shall we go,' says they, bein' a rellijous people, 'an' divvle th' sthep further.' An' they killed off th' irrelijous naygurs an' started in f'r to raise cattle. An' at night they'd set outside iv their dorps, which, Hinnissy, is Dutch f'r two-story brick house an' lot, an' sip their la-ager an' swap horses an' match texts fr'm th' Bible f'r th' seegars, while th' childer played marbles with dimons as big as th' end iv ye'er thumb.

"Well, th' English heerd they was goold be th' bucket in ivry cellar fr'm Oopencoff to Doozledorf, which, Hinnissy, is like New York an' San Francisco, bein' th' exthreme pints iv th' counthry, an' they come on in gr-reat hordes, sturdy Anglo-Saxons fr'm Saxony, th' Einsteins an' Heidlebacks an' Werners an' whin they took out goold enough so's they needed raycreation they wanted to vote. 'An',' says Joe Chamberlain, he says, 'Be hivins, they shall vote,' he says. 'Is it,' he says, 'possible that at this stage iv th' world's progress' he says, 'an English gintleman shud be denied,' he says, 'th' right to dhrop off a thrain annywhere in th' civilized wurruld an' cast his impeeryal vote?' he says. 'Give thim th' franchise,' he says, 'or be this an' be that!' he says, 'f'r we have put our hand to th' plough, an' we will not turn back,' he says.

{Illustration}

"Kruger, that's th' main guy iv th' Dutch, a fine man, Hennissy, that looks like Casey's goat an' has manny iv th' same peculyarities, he says, 'All r-right,' he says, 'I'll give thim th' franchise,' he says. 'Whin?' says Joe Chamberlain. 'In me will,' says Kruger. 'Whin I die,' he says, 'an' I hope to live to be a hundherd if I keep on smokin' befure breakfast,' he says, 'I'll bequeath to me frinds, th' English, or such iv thim as was here befure I come, th' inalienable an' sacred right to demand fr'm me succissor th' privilege iv ilictin' an aldherman,' he says. 'But,' he says, 'in th' mane-time,' he says, 'we'll lave things the way they are,' he says. 'I'm old,' he say, 'an' not good-lookin',' he says, 'an' me clothes don't fit an' they may be marks iv food on me vest,' he says, 'but I'm not more thin half crazy an' annytime ye find me givin' annywan a chanst to vote me into a job dhrivin' a mule an' put in an English prisidint iv this ray-public,' he says, 'ye may conclude that ye'er Uncle Paul needs a guarjeen!' he says.

"'Far be it fr'm me to suggist anny but peaceful measures,' says Sir Alfred Milner, that's th' lad they have down in Africa, th' Injun agent, 'f'r th' English an' Dutch shud wurruk together like brothers f'r th' removal iv th' naygur popylation,' he says, 'but,' he says, 'as a brother I politely suggest to ye that if ye don't give us what we want we'll hand ye a fraternal punch!' he says. 'F'r,' he says,' 'we have put our hand to th' plough,' he says, 'an' we cannot turn back,' he says.

"'What Sir Alfred Milner says is thrue,' says Lord Lelborne, an' what th' divvle he has to do about it I dinnaw. 'Th' situation is such,' he says, 'as to be intol'rable to a silf-rayspictin' Englishman,' he says. 'What a crime,' he says, 'that th' men who ar-re takin' most iv th' money out iv th' counthry shud not be allowed to stick in anny iv th' votes,' he says. 'We have, as Shakespeare says, put our hand to th' plough,' he says, 'an' we cannot turn back,' he says. 'I agree corjally with th' noble lord on th' r-red lounge abaft me,' says Lord Salisbury. 'With the echoes of me own noble sintimints on th' peace proclamation iv me good frind, th' Czar iv Rooshia, still ringin' in me ears,' he says, 'it wud ill become me to speak iv foorce,' he says. 'I wud on'y say that if th' Transvaal raypublic wud rather have a Dum-dum bullet in its tum-tum thin grant to Englishmen th' r-right to run th' govermint, thin th' Transvaal rapublic'll have both!' he says. 'I will add,' he says, 'that we have put our hand to th' plough an' we will not turn back,' he says.

"Well, sir, 'twas up to Kruger an' he knocked th' ashes out iv his pipe on his vest an' says he, 'Gintlemen,' he says, 'I wud like to do me best to accomydate ye,' he says. 'Nawthin' short iv a severe attack iv sickness wud plaze me so much as to see long lines iv Englishmen marchin' up to th' polls an' depositin' their ballots again' me f'r prisidint,' he says. 'But,' he says, 'I'm an old man!' he says. 'I was ilicted young an' I niver done annything since,' he says. 'I wudden't know what to do without it,' he says. 'What ye propose is to make an ex-prisidint iv me. D'ye think I cud stand that? D'ye think at my age I wud be contint to dash fr'm wan justice coort to another pleadin' f'r habyas-corpus writs or test me principles iv personal expansion in a Noo Jarsey village?' he says. 'I'd rather be a dead prisidint thin a live ex-prisidint. If I have anny pollytical ambition I'd rather be a Grant or a Garfield thin a Cleveland or a Harrison,' he says. 'I may've read it in th' Bible, though I think I saw it in a scand'lous book me frind Rhodes left in his bedroom las' time he called on me, that ye shud niver discard an ace to dhraw to a flush,' he says. 'I deplore th' language but th' sintimint is sound,' he says. 'An' I believe ye'er intintions to presarve peace ar-re honest, but I don't like to see ye pullin' off ye'er coat an' here goes f'r throuble while ye have ye'er arms in th' sleeves,' he says. 'F'r,' he says, 'ye have put ye'er hand in th' reaper an' it cannot turn back,' he says.

"An' there they go, Hinnissy. I'm not again England in this thing, Hinnissy, an' I'm not again th' Boers. Like Mack I'm divided on a matther iv principle between a desire to cemint th' 'lieance an' an affection f'r th' Dutch vote. But if Kruger had spint his life in a rale raypublic where they burn gas he cud've settled th' business without losin' sleep. If I was Kruger there'd've been no war."

"What wud ye have done?" Mr. Hennessy asked.

"I'd give thim th' votes," said Mr. Dooley. "But," he added significantly, "I'd do th' countin'."

WAR AND WAR MAKERS

"I tell ye, Hinnissy," said Mr. Dooley, "Ye can't do th' English-speakin' people. Oursilves an' th' hands acrost th' sea ar-re rapidly teachin' th' benighted Lutheryan an' other haythin that as a race we're onvincible an' oncatcheable. Th' Anglo-Saxon race meetin's now going on in th' Ph'lippeens an' South Africa ought to convince annywan that give us a fair start an' we can bate th' wurruld to a tillygraft office.

"Th' war our cousins be Sir Thomas Lipton is prosecutin', as Hogan says, again th' foul but accrate Boers is doin' more thin that. It's givin' us a common war lithrachoor. I wudden't believe at first whin I r-read th' dispatches in th' pa-apers that me frind Gin'ral Otis wasn't in South Africa. It was on'y whin I see another chapter iv his justly cillybrated seeryal story, intitled 'Th' Capture iv Porac' that I knew he had an imitator in th' mother counthry. An' be hivins, I like th' English la-ad's style almost as well as our own gr-reat artist's. Mebbe'tis, as th' pa-apers say, that Otis has writ himsilf out. Annyhow th' las' chapter isn't thrillin'. He says: 'To-day th' ar-rmy undher my command fell upon th' inimy with gr-reat slaughter an' seized th' important town of Porac which I have mintioned befure, but,' he says, 'we ar-re fortunately now safe in Manila.' Ye see he doesn't keep up th' intherest to th' end. Th' English pote does betther."

"'Las' night at eight o'clock,' he says, 'we found our slendher but inthrepid ar-rmy surrounded be wan hundhred thousan' Boers,' he says. 'We attackted thim with gr-reat fury,' he says, 'pursuin' thim up th' almost inaccessible mountain side an' capturin' eight guns which we didn't want so we give thim back to thim with siveral iv our own,' he says. 'Th' Irish rig'mints,' he says, 'th' Kerry Rifles, th' Land Leaguers' Own, an' th' Dublin Pets, commanded be th' Pop'lar Irish sojer Gin'ral Sir Ponsonby Tompkins wint into battle singin' their well-known naytional anthem: "Mrs. Innery Awkins is a fust-class name!" Th' Boers retreated,' he says, 'pursued be th' Davitt Terrors who cut their way through th' fugitives with awful slaughter,' he says. 'They have now,' he says, 'pinethrated as far us Pretoria,' he says, 'th' officers arrivin' in first-class carredges an' th' men in thrucks,' he says, 'an' ar-re camped in th' bettin' shed where they ar-re afforded ivry attintion be th' vanquished inimy,' he says. 'As f'r us,' he says, 'we decided afther th' victhry to light out f'r Ladysmith.' he says, 'Th' inimy had similar intintions,' he says, 'but their skill has been vastly overrated,' he says. 'We bate thim,' he says 'we bate thim be thirty miles,' he says. That's where we're sthrong, Hinnissy. We may get licked on th' battle field, we may be climbin' threes in th' Ph'lippeens with arrows stickin' in us like quills, as Hogan says, into th' fretful porcupine or we may be doin' a mile in five minyits flat down th' pike that leads to Cape Town pursued be th' less fleet but more ignorant Boers peltin' us with guns full iv goold an' bibles, but in th' pages iv histhry that our childhren read we niver turned back on e'er an inimy. We make our own gloryous pages on th' battlefield, in th' camp an' in th' cab'net meetin'."

"Well, 't is all r-right f'r ye to be jokin'," said Mr. Hennessy, "but there's manny a brave fellow down there that it's no joke to."

"Thrue f'r ye," said Mr. Dooley, "an' that's why I wisht it cud be fixed up so's th' men that starts th' wars could do th' fightin'. Th' throuble is that all th' prelimin'ries is arranged be matchmakers an' all they'se left f'r fighters is to do th' murdherin'. A man's got a good job at home an' he wants to make it sthronger. How can he do it? Be throwin' out some one that's got an akelly good job down th' sthreet. Now he don't go over as I wud an' say, 'Here Schwartzmeister (or Kruger as th' case may be) I don't like ye'er appearance, ye made a monkey iv me in argymint befure th' neighborhood an' if ye continyue in business ye'll hurt me thrade, so here goes to move ye into th' sthreet!' Not that la-ad. He gets a crowd around him an' says he: 'Kruger (or Schwartzmeister as th' case may be) is no good. To begin with he's a Dutchman. If that ain't enough he's a cantin', hymn singin' murdhrous wretch that wuddent lave wan iv our counthrymen ate a square meal if he had his way. I'll give ye all two dollars a week if ye'll go over an' desthroy him.' An' th' other la-ad, what does he do? He calls in th' neighbors an' says he: 'Dooley is sindin' down a gang iv savages to murdher me. Do ye lave ye'er wurruk an' ye'er families an' rally ar-round me an' where ye see me plug hat wave do ye go in th' other direction,' he says, 'an' slay th' brutal inimy,' he says. An' off goes th' sojers an' they meet a lot iv la-ads that looks like thimsilves an' makes sounds that's more or less human an' ates out iv plates an' they swap smokin' tobacco an' sings songs together an' th' next day they're up early jabbing holes in each other with baynits. An' whin its all over they'se me an' Chamberlain at home victoryous an' Kruger an' Schwartzmeister at home akelly victoryous. An' they make me prime minister or aldherman but whin I want a man to put in me coal I don't take wan with a wooden leg.

"I'll niver go down again to see sojers off to th' war. But ye'll see me at th' depot with a brass band whin th' men that causes wars starts f'r th' scene iv carnage. Whin Congress goes forth to th' sun-kissed an' rain jooled isles iv th' Passyfic no more heartier cheer will be heard thin th' wan or two that rises fr'm th' bosom iv Martin Dooley. Says I, give thim th' chanst to make histhry an' lave th' young men come home an' make car wheels. If Chamberlain likes war so much 'tis him that ought to be down there in South Africa peltin' over th' road with ol' Kruger chasin' him with a hoe. Th' man that likes fightin' ought to be willin' to turn in an' spell his fellow-counthrymen himsilf. An' I'd even go this far an' say that if Mack wants to subjoo th' dam Ph'lippeens——"

"Ye're a thraitor," said Mr. Hennessy.

"I know it," said Mr. Dooley, complacently.

"Ye're an anti-expansionist."

"If ye say that again," cried Mr. Dooley, angrily, "I'll smash in ye'er head."

UNDERESTIMATING THE ENEMY

"What d'ye think iv th' war?" Mr. Hennessy asked.

"I think I want to go out an' apologize to Shafter," said Mr. Dooley.

"I'm like ivrybody else, be hivins, I thought war was like shootin' glass balls. I niver thought iv th' glass balls thrainin' a dinnymite gun on me. 'Tis a thrait iv us Anglo-Saxons that we look on an inimy as a target. If ye hit him ye get three good see-gars. We're like people that dhreams iv fights. In me dhreams I niver lost wan fight. A man I niver saw befure comes up an' says something mane to me, that I can't raymimber, an' I climb into him an' 'tis all over in a minyit. He niver hits me, or if he does I don't feel it. I put him on his back an' bate him to death. An' thin I help mesilf to his watch an' chain an' me frinds come down an' say, 'Martin, ye haven't a scratch,' an' con-grathlate me, an' I wandher ar-roun' th' shtreets with a chip on me shoulder till I look down an' see that I haven't a stitch on me but a short shirt. An' thin I wake up. Th' list iv knock-outs to me credit in dhreams wud make Fitzsimmons feel poor. But ne'er a wan iv thim was printed in th' pa-apers."

"'Tis so with me frinds, th' hands acrost th' sea. They wint to sleep an' had a dhream. An' says they: 'We will sind down to South Africa thim gallant throops that have won so manny hard-fought reviews,' they says, 'captained,' they says, 'be th' flower iv our aristocracy,' they says. 'An' whin th' Boers come out ar-rmed with rollin' pins an' bibles,' they says, 'We'll just go at thim,' they says, 'an' walk through thim an' that night we'll have a cotillyon at Pretoria to which all frinds is invited,' they says. An' so they deposit their intellects in th' bank at home, an' th' absent-minded beggars goes out in thransports iv pathreetism an' pothry. An' they'se a meetin' iv th' cabinet an' 'tis decided that as th' war will on'y las' wan week 'twill be well f'r to begin renamin' th' cities iv th' Thransvaal afther pop'lar English statesmen—Joechamberlainville an' Rhodesdorp an' Beitfontein. F'r they have put their hands to th' plough an' th' sponge is squeezed dhry, an' th' sands iv th' glass have r-run out an' th' account is wiped clean."

"An' what's th' Boer doin' all this time? What's me frind th' Boer doin'. Not sleepin', Hinnissy, mind ye. He hasn't anny dhreams iv conquest. But whin a man with long whiskers comes r-ridin' up th' r-road an' says: 'Jan Schmidt or Pat O'Toole or whativer his name is, ye're wanted at th' front,' he goes home an' takes a rifle fr'm th' wall an' kisses his wife an' childher good-bye an' puts a bible in th' tails iv his coat an' a stovepipe hat on his head an' thramps away.

An' his wife says: 'Good-bye, Jan. Don't be long gone an' don't get shooted.' An' he says: 'Not while I've got a leg undher me an' a rock in front iv me,' he says. I tell ye, Hinnissy, ye can't beat a man that fights fr his home an' counthry in a stovepipe hat. He might be timpted fr to come out fr'm cover fr his native land, but he knows if he goes home to his wife with his hat mussed she won't like it, an' so he sets behind a rock an' plugs away. If th' lid is knocked off he's fatally wounded."

"What's th' raysult, Hinnissy? Th' British marches up with their bands playin' an' their flags flyin'. An' th' Boers squat behind a bouldher or a three or set comfortable in th' bed iv a river an' bang away. Their on'y thradition is that it's betther to be a live Boer thin a dead hero, which comes, perhaps, to th' same thing. They haven't been taught fr hundherds iv years that 'tis a miracle fr to be an officer an' a disgrace to be a private sojer. They know that if they're kilt they'll have their names printed in th' pa-apers as well as th' Markess iv Doozleberry that's had his eyeglass shot out. But they ain't lookin' fr notoriety. All they want is to get home safe, with their counthry free, their honor protected an' their hats in good ordher. An' so they hammer away an' th' inimy keeps comin', an' th' varyous editions iv th' London pa-apers printed in this counthry have standin' a line iv type beginnin', 'I regret to state.'"

"All this, Hinnissy, comes fr'm dhreamin' dhreams. If th' British had said, 'This unclean an' raypeecious people that we're against is also very tough. Dirty though they be, they'll fight. Foul though their nature is, they have ca'tridges in their belts. This not bein' England an' th' inimy we have again us not bein' our frinds, we will frget th' gloryous thraditions iv th' English an' Soudan ar-rmies an' instead iv r-rushin' on thim sneak along yon kindly fence an' hit thim on th' back iv th' neck,'—they'd be less, 'I r-regret-to-states' and more 'I'm plazed-to-reports.' They wud so, an' I'm a man that's been through columns an' columns iv war. Ye'll find, Hinnissy, that 'tis on'y ar-rmies fights in th' open. Nations fights behind threes an' rocks. Ye can put that in ye're little book. 'Tis a sayin' I made as I wint along."

"We done th' same way oursilves," said Mr. Hennessy.

"We did that," said Mr. Dooley. "We were in a dhream, too. Th' on'y thing is th' other fellow was in a thrance. We woke up first. An' anny-how I'm goin' to apologize to Shafter. He may not have anny medals fr standin' up in range iv th' guns but, be hivins, he niver dhrove his buckboard into a river occypied be th' formerly loathed Castile."

THE WAR EXPERT

Mr. Dooley was reading the war news—not our war news but the war news we are interested in—when Mr. Hennessy interrupted him to ask "What's a war expert?"

"A war expert," said Mr. Dooley, "is a man ye niver heerd iv befure. If ye can think iv annywan whose face is onfamilyar to ye an' ye don't raymimber his name, an' he's got a job on a pa-aper ye didn't know was published, he's a war expert. 'Tis a har-rd office to fill. Whin a war begins th' timptation is sthrong f'r ivry man to grab hold iv a gun an go to th' fr-ront. But th' war expert has to subjoo his cravin' f'r blood. He says to himsilf 'Lave others seek th' luxuries iv life in camp,' he says. 'F'r thim th' boat races acrost th' Tugela, th' romp over the kopje, an' th' game iv laager, laager who's got th' laager?' he says. 'I will stand be me counthry,' he says, 'close,' he says. 'If it falls,' he says, 'it will fall on me,' he says. An' he buys himsilf a map made be a fortune teller in a dhream, a box iv pencils an' a field glass, an' goes an' looks f'r a job as a war expert. Says th' editor iv th' pa-aper: 'I don't know ye. Ye must be a war expert,' he says. 'I am,' says th' la-ad. 'Was ye iver in a war?' says th' editor. 'I've been in nawthin' else,' says th' la-ad. 'Durin' th' Spanish-American War, I held a good job as a dhramatic critic in Dedham, Matsachoosets,' he says. 'Whin th' bullets flew thickest in th' Soodan I was spoortin' editor iv th' Christyan Advocate,' he says. 'I passed through th' Franco-Prooshan War an' held me place, an' whin th' Turks an' Rooshans was at each other's throats, I used to lay out th' campaign ivry day on a checker board,' he says. 'War,' he says, has no turrors f'r me,' he says. 'Ye're th man f'r th' money,' says th' editor. An' he gets th' job."

"Thin th' war breaks out in earnest. No matther how manny is kilt, annything that happens befure th' war expert gets to wurruk is on'y what we might call a prelimin'ry skirmish. He sets down an' bites th' end iv his pencil an' looks acrost th' sthreet an' watches a man paintin' a sign. Whin th' man gets through he goes to th' window an' waits to see whether th' polisman that wint into th' saloon is afther a dhrink or sarvin' a warrant. If he comes r-right out 'tis a warrant. Thin he sets back in a chair an' figures out that th' pitchers on th' wall pa-aper ar-re all alike ivry third row. Whin his mind is thurly tuned up be these inthricate problems, he dashes to his desk an' writes what you an' I read th' nex' day in th' pa-apers."

"Clarence Pontoon, th' military expert iv th' London Mornin' Dhram, reviewin' Gin'ral Buller's position on th' Tugela, says: 'It is manifest fr'm th' dispatches tellin' that Gin'ral Buller has crost th' Tugela River that Gin'ral Buller has crost th' Tugela River. This we r-read in spite iv th' cinsor. Th' question is which side he has crost to. On Friday he was on th' north side in th' mornin' an' on th' south side at night, an' in th' river at noon. We heerd nawthin' Sathurdah mornin'. Th' presumption is that they was nawthin' to hear. Therefore it is aisy to imagine Gin'ral Buller, findin' his position on th' north side ontenable an' his position on th' south side onbearable, is thransportin' his troops up th' river on rafts an' is now engagin' th' inimy between Spitzozone an' Rottenfontein, two imminsely sthrong points. All this dimonsthrates th' footility an' foolishness iv attimptin' to carry a frontal position agains' large, well-fed Dutchmen with mud in th' fr-ront iv thim."

"'I cal'clate that it wud require thirty millyon thurly dauntless Britions to ixicute such a manoover, tin Boers ar-rmed with pop bottles bein' now considhered th' akel iv a brigade. What I wud do if I was Buller, an' I thank Hivin I'm not, wud be move me ar-rmy in half-an-hour over th' high but aisily accessible mountains to th' right iv Crowrijoy's forces, an' takin' off me shoes so he cudden't hear thim squeak, creep up behind th' Dutch an' lam their heads off. Afther this sthroke 'twud be aisy f'r to get th' foorces iv Fr-rinch, Gatacre, Methoon, an' Winston Churchill together some afthernoon, invite th' inimy to a band concert, surround an' massacree thim. This adroit move cud be ixicuted if Roberts wud on'y make use iv th' ixicillint bus sarvice between Hokesmith an' Mikesmith. It is exthraordinary that th' gin'ral on th' groun' has not seen th' possibilities so apparent at a distance.'"

"That's wan kind iv war expert, Hinnissy. Another kind is th' wan that gives it good to th' gover'mint. Says Willum McGlue, war expert iv th' London Mornin' Growl, who's supposed to be cheek be jowl with Lord Wolseley. 'England's greatness is slippin' away. Th' failure iv th' gover'mint to provide a well-equipped, thurly pathriotic ar-rmy iv Boers to carry on this war undher th' leadership iv gallant Joobert is goin' to be our roonation. We ar-re bethrayed be a lazy, effete, side-whiskered, golf-playin' gover'mint that wud rather lose this fight thin win it because they ar-re tired iv holdin' office. What can be said f'r public men so lost to shame that they spell Kopje with a "c" an' ar-re sindin' Englishmen to th' ends iv th' wurruld to fight f'r England? Down with thim!'"

"Well sir, 'tis a gr-reat thing f'r a counthry to have th' likes iv thim ar-round to direct manoovers that'd be gatherin' dust on th' shelf if th' gin'rals had their say, an' to prove to th' wurruld that th' English ar-re not frivolous, excitable people like us an' th' Frinch, but can take a batin' without losin' their heads."

"Sure," said Mr. Hennessy, "tis not thim that does th' fightin'. Th' la-ads with th' guns has that job."

"Well," said Mr. Dooley, "they'se two kinds iv fightin'. Th' experts wants th' arrmy to get into Pretoria dead or alive, an' th' sojers wants to get in alive. I'm no military expert, Hinnissy. I'm too well known. But I have me own opinyon on th' war. All this talk about th' rapid fire gun an' modhren methods iv warfare makes me wondher. They'se not so much diff'rence between war now an' war whin I was a kid, as they let on. Th' gun that shoots ye best fr'm a distance don't shoot ye so well close to. A pile iv mud is a pile iv mud now just th' same as it was whin Gin'ral Grant was pokin' ar-round. If th' British can get over th' mud pile they win th' fight. If they can't they're done. That's all they'se to it. Mos' men, sthrongest backs, best eyes an' th' ownership iv th' mud piles. That's war, Hinnissy. Th' British have th' men. They're shy iv backs, eyes an' mud piles, an' they will be until they larn that sheep-herdin' an' gin'ralship ar-re diff'rent things, an' fill up their ar-rmy with men that ar-re not fightin' f'r money or glory, but because they want to get home to their wives alive."

"Ye talk like an' ol book," said Mr. Hennessy, in disgust. "Ye with ye-re maundhrin' ar-re no betther thin thim expert la-ads."

"Well annyhow," said Mr. Dooley thoughtfully, "th' expert is sarvin' a useful purpose. Th' papers says th' rapid fire gun'll make war in th' future impossible. I don't think that, but I know th' expert will."

MODERN EXPLOSIVES

"If iver I wanted to go to war," said Mr. Dooley, "an' I niver did, th' desire has passed fr'm me iv late. Ivry time I read iv th' desthructive power iv modhern explosives col' chills chase each other up an' down me spine."

"What's this here stuff they calls lyddite?" Mr. Hennessy asked.

"Well, 'tis th' divvle's own med'cine," said Mr. Dooley. "Compared with lyddite joynt powdher is Mrs. Winslow's soothin' surup, an' ye cud lave th' childher play base-ball with a can iv dinnymite. 'Tis as sthrong as Gin'ral Crownjoy's camp th' day iv th' surrinder an' almost as sthrong as th' pollytics iv Montana. Th' men that handles it is cased in six inch armor an' played on be a hose iv ice wather. Th' gun that shoots it is always blown up be th' discharge. Whin this deadly missile flies through th' air, th' threes ar-re withered an' th' little bur-rds falls dead fr'm th' sky, fishes is kilt in th' rivers, an' th' tillyphone wires won't wurruk. Th' keen eyed British gunners an' corryspondints watches it in its hellish course an' tur-rn their faces as it falls into th' Boer trench. An' oh! th' sickly green fumes it gives off, jus' like pizen f'r potato bugs! There is a thremenjous explosion. Th' earth is thrown up f'r miles. Horses, men an' gun carredges ar-re landed in th' British camp whole. Th' sun is obscured be Boer whiskers turned green. Th' heart iv th' corryspondint is made sick be th' sight, an' be th' thought iv th' fearful carnage wrought be this dhread desthroyer in th' ranks iv th' brave but misguided Dutchmen. Th' nex' day deserters fr'm th' Boer ranks reports that they have fled fr'm th' camp, needin' a dhrink an' onable to stand th' scenes iv horror. They announce that th' whole Boer ar-rmy is as green as wall paper, an' th' Irish brigade has sthruck because ye can't tell their flag fr'm th' flag iv th' r-rest iv th' Dutch. Th' Fr-rinch gin'ral in command iv th' Swedish corps lost his complexion an' has been sint to th' hospital, an' Mrs. Gin'ral Crownjoy's washin' that was hangin' on th' line whin th' bombardmint comminced is a total wreck which no amount iv bluin' will save. Th' deserters also report that manny iv th' Boers ar-re outspannin', trekkin', loogerin', kopjein' an' veldtin' home to be dyed, f'r'tis not known whether lyddite is a fast color or will come out in th' wash."

"In spite iv their heavy losses th' Boers kept up a fierce fire. They had no lyddite, but with their other divvlish modhern explosives they wrought thremenjous damage. F'r some hours shells burst with turr'ble precision in th' British camp. Wan man who was good at figures counted as manny as forty-two thousan' eight hundhred an' sivin burstin' within a radyus iv wan fut. Ye can imagine th' hor-rible carnage. Colonel C. G. F. K. L. M. N. O. P.

Hetherington-Casey-Higgins lost his eye-glass tin times, th' las' time almost swallowin' it, while ye'er faithful corryspondint was rindered deaf be th' explosions. Another Irish rig'mint has disappearded, th' Twelve Thousandth an' Eighth, Dublin Fusiliers. Brave fellows, 'tis suspected they mistook th' explosion of lyddite f'r a Pathrick's Day procession an' wint acrost to take a look at it."

"Murdher, but 'tis dhreadful to r-read about. We have to change all our conciptions iv warfare. Wanst th' field was r-red, now 'tis a br-right lyddite green. Wanst a man wint out an' died f'r his counthry, now they sind him out an' lyddite dyes him. What do I mane? 'Tis a joke I made. I'll not explane it to ye. Ye wudden't undherstand it. 'Tis f'r th' eddycated classes."

"How they're iver goin' to get men to fight afther this I cudden't tell ye. 'Twas bad enough in th' ol' days whin all that happened to a sojer was bein' pinithrated be a large r-round gob iv solder or stuck up on th' end iv a baynit be a careless inimy. But now-a-days, they have th' bullet that whin it enthers ye tur-rns ar-round like th' screw iv a propeller, an' another wan that ye might say goes in be a key-hole an' comes out through a window, an' another that has a time fuse in it an' it doesn't come out at all but stays in ye, an' mebbe twinty years afther, whin ye've f'rgot all about it an' ar-re settin' at home with ye'er fam'ly, bang! away it goes an' ye with it, carryin' off half iv th' roof. Thin they have guns as long as fr'm here to th' rollin' mills that fires shells as big as a thrunk. Th' shells are loaded like a docthor's bag an' have all kinds iv things in thim that won't do a bit iv good to man or beast. If a sojer has a weak back there's something in th' shell that removes a weak back; if his head throubles him, he can lose it; if th' odher iv vilets is distasteful to him th' shell smothers him in vilet powdher. They have guns that anny boy or girl who knows th' typewriter can wurruk, an' they have other guns on th' music box plan, that ye wind up an' go away an' lave, an' they annoy anny wan that comes along. They have guns that bounces up out iv a hole in th' groun', fires a millyon shells a minyit an' dhrops back f'r another load. They have guns that fire dinnymite an' guns that fire th' hateful, sickly green lyddite that makes th' inimy look like fiat money, an' guns that fire canned beef f'r th' inimy an' distimper powdher for th' inimy's horses. An' they have some guns that shoot straight."

"Well, thin," Mr. Hennessy grumbled, "it's a wondher to me that with all thim things they ain't more people kilt. Sure, Gin'ral Grant lost more men in wan day thin th' British have lost in four months, an' all he had to keep tab on was ol' fashioned bullets an' big, bouncin' iron balls."

"Thrue," said Mr. Dooley. "I don't know th' reason, but it mus' be that th' betther gun a man has th' more he thrusts th' gun an' th' less he thrusts himsilf. He stays away an' shoots. He says to himsilf, he says: 'They'se nawthin' f'r me to do,' he says, 'but load up me little lyddite cannon with th' green goods,' he says, 'an' set here at the organ,' he says, 'pull out th' stops an' paint th' town iv Pretoria green,' he says. 'But,' he says, 'on sicond thought, suppose th' inimy shud hand it back to me,' he says. 'Twud be oncomfortable,' he says. 'So,' he says, 'I'll jus' move me music back a mile,' he says, 'an' peg away, an' th' longest gun takes th' persimmons,' he says. 'Tis this way: If ye an' I fall out an' take rifles to each other, 'tis tin to wan nayether iv us gets clost enough to hit. If we take pistols th' odds is rayjooced. If we take swords I may get a hack at ye, but if we take a half-nelson lock 'tis even money I have ye'er back broke befure th' polis comes."

"I can see in me mind th' day whin explosives'll be so explosive an' guns'll shoot so far that on'y th' folks that stay at home'll be kilt, an' life insurance agents'll be advisin' people to go into th' ar-rmy. I can so. 'Tis thrue what Hogan says about it."

"What's that?" Mr. Hennessy asked.

"Th' nation," said Mr. Dooley, "that fights with a couplin' pin extinds its bordhers at th' cost iv th' nation that fights with a clothes pole."

"Well, sir," said Mr. Dooley, "'tis a fine rayciption th' Boer dillygates is havin' in this counthry."

"They'll be out here nex' week," said Mr. Hennessy.

"They will that," Mr. Dooley replied, "an' we'll show thim that our inthrest in small raypublics fightin' f'r their liberty ain't disappeared since we become an impeeryal nation. No, sir. We have as much inthrest as iver, but we have more inthrests elsewhere."

"Oom Paul, he says to th' la-ads: 'Go,' he says, 'to me good an' great frind, Mack th' Wanst, an' lay th' case befure him,' he says. 'Tell him,' he says, 'that th' situation is just th' same as it was durin' Wash'nton's time,' he says, 'on'y Wash'nton won, an' we're rapidly losin' kopjes till we soon won't have wan to sthrike a match on,' he says. An' off goes th' good men. Whin they started the Boers was doin' pretty well, Hinnissy. They were fightin' Englishmen, an' that's a lawn tinnis to a rale fightin' man. But afther awhile the murdherin' English gover'mint put in a few recreent but gallant la-ads fr'm th' ol' dart—we ought to be proud iv thim, curse thim—Pat O'Roberts, an' Mike McKitchener, an' Terrence O'Fr-rinch—an' they give th' view—halloo an' wint through th' Dutch like a party comin' home fr'm a fifteenth iv August picnic might go through a singerbund. So be th' time th' dillygates got to Europe it was: 'James, if thim br-rave but misguided Dutch appears, squirt th' garden hose on thim. I'll see th' British embassadure this afthernoon.' Ye see, Hinnissy, 'twas ol' Kruger's play to keep on winnin' battles till th' dillygates had their say. Th' amount iv sympathy that goes out fr a sthrugglin' people is reg'lated, Hinnissy, be th' amount iv sthrugglin' th' people can do. Th' wurruld, me la-ad, is with th' undher dog on'y as long as he has a good hold an' a chanst to tur-rn over."

"Well, sir, whin th' dillygates see they cudden't do business in Europe, says they to thimsilves: 'We'll pike acrost th' ragin' sea,' they says, 'an in th' home iv Wash'nton, Lincoln, an' Willum J. Bryan, ye bet we'll have a hearin',' an' they got wan. Ivrybody's listenin' to thim. But no wan replies. If they'd come here three months ago, befure Crownjoy was suffocated out iv his hole in th' groun', they'd be smokin' their pipes in rockin' chairs on th' veranda iv th' white house an' passin' th' bucket between thim an' Mack. But 'tis diff'rent now. 'Tis diff'rent now. Says Willum J. Bryan: 'I can't see thim mesilf, fr it may not be long befure I'll have to dale with these inthricate problems, I hope an' pray, but Congressman Squirtwather, do ye disguise ye'ersilf as a private citizen an' go down to th' hotel an' tell these la-ads that I'm with thim quietly if public opinyon justifies it an' Mack takes th' other side. Tell thim I frequently say to mesilf that they're all r-right, but I wudden't want it to go further. Perhaps they cud be injooced to speak at a dimmycratic meetin' unbeknown to me,' he says.

"Sicrety Hay meets thim in a coal cellar, wearin' a mask. 'Gintlemen,' says he, 'I can assure ye th' prisidint an' mesilf feels mos' deeply fr ye. I needn't tell ye about mesilf,' he says. 'Haven't I sint me own son into ye'er accursed but liberty-lovin' counthry,' he says. 'As fr Mack, I assure ye he's hear-rtbroken over th' tur-rn affairs have taken,' he says. 'Early in th' war he wrote to Lord Salisberry, sayin' he hoped 'twud not be continyued to iliction day, an' Salisberry give him a gruff response. Tur-rned him down, though both ar-re Anglo-Saxons,' he says. 'Las' night his sobs fairly shook th' white house as he thought iv ye an' ye'er sthruggle. He wants to tell ye how much he thinks iv ye, an' he'll meet ye in th' carredge house if ye'll shave off ye'er whiskers an' go as clam-peddlers. Ye'll reco'nize him in a green livery. He'll wear a pink carnation in his buttonhole. Give th' names iv Dorsey an' Flannagan, an' if th' English ambassadure goes by get down on ye'er ban's an' knees an' don't make a sign till he's out iv sight,' he says. 'Th' stout party in blue near by'll be Mark Hanna. He may be able to arrange a raypublican meetin' f'r ye to addhress,' he says. 'The gr-reat hear-rt iv th' raypublican party throbs f'r ye. So does Mack's,' he says. 'So does mine,' he says."

"Well, th' dillygates met Mack an' they had a pleasant chat. 'Will ye,' says they, 'inthervene an' whistle off th' dogs iv war?' they says. 'Whisper,' says Mack, th' tears flowin' down his cheeks. 'Iver since this war started me eyes have been fixed on th' gallant or otherwise, nation or depindancy, fightin' its brave battle f'r freedom or rebellin' again' th' sov'reign power, as the case may be,' he says. 'Unofficially, my sympathy has gone out to ye, an' bur-rnin' wurruds iv unofficial cheer has been communicated unofficially be me to me official fam'ly, not, mind ye, as an official iv this magnificent an' liberty-lovin' raypublic, but as a private citizen,' he says. 'I feel, as a private citizen, that so long,' he says, 'as the br-right star iv liberty shines resplindent over our common counthries, with th' example iv Washin'ton in ye'er eyes, an' th' iliction comin' on, that ye must go forward an' conker or die,' he says. 'An',' he says, 'Willum McKinley is not th' man to put annything in ye'er way,' he says. 'Go back to me gr-reat an' good frind an' tell him that th' hear-rt iv th' raypublican party throbs f'r him,' he says. 'An' Sicrety Hay's,' he says, 'an' mine,' he says, 'unofficially,' he says. 'Me official hear-rt,' he says, 'is not permitted be th' constitootion to throb durin' wurrukin' hours,' he says.

"An' so it goes. Ivrywhere th' dillygates tur-rns they see th' sign: 'This is me busy day.' An' whin they get back home they can tell th' people they found th' United States exudin' sympathy at ivry pore—'marked private.'"

"Don't ye think th' United States is enthusyastic f'r th' Boers?" asked the innocent Hennessy.

"It was," said Mr. Dooley. "But in th' las' few weeks it's had so manny things to think iv. Th' enthusyasm iv this counthry, Hinnissy, always makes me think iv a bonfire on an ice-floe. It burns bright so long as ye feed it, an' it looks good, but it don't take hold, somehow, on th' ice."

THE CHINESE SITUATION

"Well, sir," said Mr. Hennessy, "to think iv th' audacity iv thim Chinymen! It do bate all."

"It do that," said Mr. Dooley. "It bates th' wurruld. An' what's it comin' to? You an' me looks at a Chinyman as though he wasn't good fr annything but washin' shirts, an' not very good at that. Tis wan iv th' spoorts iv th' youth iv our gr-reat cities to rowl an impty beer keg down th' steps iv a Chinee laundhry, an' if e'er a Chinyman come out to resint it they'd take him be th' pigtail an' do th' joynt swing with him. But th' Chinyman at home's a diff'rent la-ad. He's with his frinds an' they're manny iv thim an' he's rowlin' th' beer kegs himsilf an' Westhren Civilization is down in th' laundhry wondhrin' whin th' police'll come along."

"Th' Lord f'rgive fr sayin' it, Hinnissy, but if I was a Chinyman, which I will fight anny man fr sayin,' an' was livin' at home, I'd tuck me shirt into me pants, put me braid up in a net, an' go out an' take a fall out iv th' in-vader if it cost me me life. Here am I, Hop Lung Dooley, r-runnin' me little liquor store an' p'rhaps raisin' a family in th' town iv Koochoo. I don't like foreigners there anny more thin I do here. Along comes a bald-headed man with chin whiskers from Baraboo, Wisconsin, an' says he: 'Benighted an' haythen Dooley,' says he, 'ye have no God,' he says. 'I have,' says I. 'I have a lot iv thim,' says I. 'Ye ar-re an oncultivated an' foul crather,' he says. 'I have come six thousan' miles fr to hist ye fr'm th' mire iv ignorance an' irrellijon in which ye live to th' lofty plane iv Baraboo,' he says. An' he sets down on an aisy chair, an' his wife an' her friends come in an' they inthrojooce Mrs. Dooley to th' modhren improvements iv th' corset an' th' hat with th' blue bur-rd onto it, an' put shame into her because she hasn't let her feet grow, while th' head mission'ry reads me a pome out iv th' *Northwesthren Christyan Advocate*. 'Well,' says I, 'look here, me good fellow,' I says. 'Me an' me people has occupied these here primises fr manny years,' I says, 'an' here we mean to stay,' I says. 'We're doin' th' best we can in th' matther iv gods,' says I. 'We have thim cast at a first-rate foundhry,' I says, 'an' we sandpa-aper thim ivry week,' says I. 'As fr knowin' things,' I says, 'me people wrote pomes with a markin' brush whin th' likes iv ye was r-runnin' ar-round wearin' a short pelisse iv sheepskins an' batin' each other to death with stone hammers,' says I. An' I'm fr firin' him out, but bein' a quite man I lave him stay."

"Th' nex' day in comes a man with a suit iv clothes that looks like a tablecloth in a section house, an' says he: 'Poor ignorant haythen,' he says, 'what manner iv food d'ye ate?' he says. 'Rice,' says I, 'an' rats is me fav'rite dish,' I says. 'Deluded wretch,' says he. 'I riprisint Armour an' Company, an' I'm here to make ye change ye'er dite,' he says. 'Hinceforth ye'll ate th' canned roast beef iv merry ol' stock yards or I'll have a file iv sojers in to fill ye full iv ondygistible lead,' he says. An' afther him comes th' man with Aunt Miranda's Pan Cakes an' Flaked Bran an' Ye'll-perish-if-ye-don't-eat-a-biscuit an' other riprisintatives iv Westhern Civilization, an' I'm to be shot if I don't take thim all."

"Thin a la-ad runs down with a chain an' a small glass on three sticks an' a gang iv section men that answers to th' name iv Casey, an' pro-ceeds fr to put down a railroad. 'What's this fr?' says I. 'We ar-re th' advance guard iv Westhren Civilization,' he says, 'an we're goin' to give ye a railroad so ye can go swiftly to places that ye don't want to see,' he says. 'A counthry that has no railroads is beneath contimpt,' he says. 'Casey,' he says,'sthretch th' chain acrost yon graveyard,' he says. 'I aim fr to put th' thrack just befure that large tombstone marked Riquiescat in Pace, James H. Chung-a-lung,' he says. 'But,' says I, 'ye will disturb pah's bones,' says I, 'if ye go to layin' ties,' I says. 'Ye'll be mixin' up me ol' man with th' Cassidy's in th' nex' lot that,' I says, 'he niver spoke to save in anger in his life,' I says. 'Ye're an ancestor worshiper, heathen,' says the la-ad, an' he goes on to tamp th' mounds in th' cimitry an ballast th' thrack with th' remains iv th' deceased. An' afther he's got through along comes a Fr-rinchman, an' an Englishman, an' a Rooshan, an' a Dutchman, an' says wan iv them: 'This is a comfortable lookin' saloon,' he says. 'I'll take th' bar, ye take th' ice-box an' th' r-rest iv th' fixtures.' 'What fr?' says I. 'I've paid th' rent an' th' license,' says I. 'Niver mind,' says he. 'We're th' riprisintatives iv Westhren Civilization,' he says, 'an' 'tis th' business iv Westhren Civilization to cut up th' belongings iv Easthren Civilization,' he says. 'Be off,' he says, 'or I'll pull ye'er hair,' he says. 'Well,' says I, 'this thing has gone far enough,' I says. 'I've heerd me good ol' cast-iron gods or josses abused,' I says, 'an' I've been packed full iv canned goods, an' th' Peking Lightnin' Express is r-runnin' sthraight through th' lot where th' bones iv me ancesthors lies,' I says. 'I've shtud it all,' I says, 'but whin ye come here to bounce me off iv me own primises,' I says, 'I'll have to take th' leg iv th' chair to ye,' I says. An' we're to th' flure."

"That's th' way it stands in Chiny, Hinnissy, an' it looks to me as though Westhren Civilization was in fr a bump. I mind wanst whin a dhrunk prize fighter come up th' r-road and wint to sleep on Slavin's steps. Some iv th' good sthrong la-ads happened along an' they were near bein' at blows over who shud have his watch an' who shud take his hat. While they were debatin' he woke up an' begin cuttin' loose with hands an' feet, an' whin he got through he made a collection iv th' things they dhropped in escapin' an' marched ca'mly down th' sthreet. Mebbe 'twill tur-rn out so in Chiny, Hinnissy. I see be th' pa-apers that they'se four hundherd millyons iv thim boys an' be hivins! 'twuddent surprise me if whin they got through batin' us at home, they might say to thimsilves: 'Well, here goes f'r a jaunt ar-roun' the wurruld.' Th' time may come, Hinnissey, whin ye'll be squirtin' wather over Hop Lee's shirt while a man named Chow Fung kicks down ye'er sign an' heaves rocks through ye'er windy. The time may come, Hinnissy. Who knows?"

"End ye'er blather," said Mr. Hennessy. "They won't be anny Chinymen left whin Imp'ror Willum gets through."

"Mebbe not," says Mr. Dooley. "He's a sthrong man. But th' Chinymen have been on earth a long time, an' I don't see how we can push so manny iv thim off iv it. Annyhow, 'tis a good thing f'r us they ain't Christyans an' haven't larned properly to sight a gun."

MINISTER WU

"Well, sir, me little Chinee frind Woo must be havin' th' time iv his life in Wash'nton these warm days," said Mr. Dooley.

"Who's he?" asked Mr. Hennessy.

"He's th' Chinee ministher," said Mr. Dooley, "an' his business is f'r to supply fresh hand-laundhried misinformation to the sicrety iv state. Th' sicrety iv state is settin' in his office feelin' blue because he's just heerd be a specyal corryspondint iv th' London Daily Pail at Sydney, Austhreelya, who had it fr'm a slatewriter in Duluth that an ar-rmy iv four hundherd an' eight thousan' millyon an' sivinty-five bloodthirsty Chinee, ar-rmed with flatirnes an' cryin', 'Bung Loo!' which means, Hinnissy, 'Kill th' foreign divvles, dhrive out th' missionries, an' set up in Chiny a gover'mint f'r the Chinee,' is marchin' on Vladivostook in Siberyia, not far fr'm Tinsin."

A knock comes at th' dure an' Woo enthers. 'Well,' says he, with a happy smile, "tis all right.' 'What's all right?' says the sicrety iv state. 'Ivrything,' says Woo. 'I have just found a letter sewed in a shirt fr'm me frind Lie Much, th' viceroy iv Bumbang. It is dated th' fourth hour iv th' third day iv th' eighth or green-cheese moon,' he says. 'What day is that?' says the sicrety iv state. 'It's Choosdah, th' fourth iv July; Winsdah, th' eighth iv October, an' Thursdah, the sivinteenth iv March,' he says. 'Pathrick's day,' says th' sicrety iv state. 'Thrue f'r ye,' says Woo. 'What year?' says Jawn Hay. 'The year iv th' big wind,' says Woo. 'Good,' says John Hay, 'proceed with ye'er story.' 'Here's th' letther,' says Woo. 'I know 'tis genooyine because it is an ol' dhress patthern used be th' impress. It says: 'Oscar Woo, care iv himsilf, annywhere: Dear Woo, brother iv th' moon, uncle iv th' sun, an' roommate iv th' stars, dear sir: Yours iv th' eighth day iv th' property moon rayceived out iv th' air yesterdah afthernoon or to-morrow, an' was glad to note ye ar-re feelin' well. Ivrything over here is th' same ol' pair iv boots. Nawthin' doin'. Peking is as quiet as th' gr-rave. Her majesty, th' impress, is sufferin' slightly fr'm death be poison, but is still able to do th' cookin' f'r the Rooshan ambassadure. Th' impror was beheaded las' week an' feels so much betther f'r the op'ration that he expicts to be quarthered nex' Sundah. He's always wanted to rayjooce his weight. Some iv th' Boxers called on th' foreigners at Tinsin las' week an' met a warrum rayciption. Th' foreigners aftherward paid a visit to thim through a hole in th' wall, an' a jolly day concluded with a foot race, at which our people are becomin' expert. Some iv th' boys expicts to come up to Peking nex' week, an' th' people along th' line iv th' railroad are gettin' ready f'r thim. This is really all the news I have, excipt that cherries ar-re ripe. Me pin is poor, me ink is dhry, me love f'r you can niver die. Give me regards to Sicrety Hay whin he wakes up. I remain, illusthrus cousin iv th' risin' dawn, thruly ye'ers, Li.

P. S.—If ye need anny more information take a longer dhraw.'

"'That,' says Woo, 'is wan way iv r-readin' it. Read upside down it says that the impress has become a Swedenboorjan. I will r-read it standin' on me head whin I get home where I can pin down me overskirt; thin I'll r-read it in a lookin' glass; thin I'll saw it into sthrips an' r-run it through a wringer an' lave it stand in a tub iv bluein', an' whin its properly starched I'll find out what it says. Fin'lly I'll cut it into small pieces an' cook with rice an' lave it to rest in a cool place, an' thin 'twill r-read even betther. I hope ye're satisfied,' he says. 'I am,' says Jawn Hay. 'I'll tillygraft to Mark that ivrything is all r-right,' he says, 'an' that our relations with his majesty or her majesty or their Boxerships or th' Down-with-th'-foreign-divvlers or whoiver's runnin' th' shop over beyant are as they ought to be or worse or betther, as th' case may be,' he says. 'Good,' says Woo, 'ye're a man afther me own heart,' he says. 'I'll sind ye a little book wrote be a frind iv mine in Peking,' he says. ''Tis called "Heart to Heart Lies I Have Had," he says. 'Ye'll like it,' he says. 'In the manetime,' he says, 'I must write a secret message to go out be to-night's hot-air express to me corryspondint in Meriden, Connecticut, urgin' him to sind more im-peeryal edicks iv a fav'r-able nature,' he says. 'I've on'y had twenty so far, an' I'm gettin' scrivener's palsy,' he says. 'But befure I go,' he says, 'I bet ye eight millyon yens, or three dollars an' eighty-four cints iv ye'er money, that ye can't pick out th' shell this here pea is undher,' he says. An' they set down to a game iv what is known at Peking as diplomacy, Hinnissy, but on Randolph sthreet viadock is called the double dirty."

"I don't believe wan wurrud iv what's in th' pa-apers about Chiny," said Mr. Hennessy.

"Well," said Mr. Dooley, "if ye believe annything ye'll believe ivrything. 'Tis a grand contist that's goin' on between Westhren an' Easthren civilliezation. 'Tis a joke iv me own, Hinnissy, an' ye'd undherstand it if ye knew spellin. Th' Westhren civilization, Hinnissy—that's us—is a pretty good liar, but he's a kind iv rough-an'-tumble at it. He goes in head down, an' ivry lie he tells looks like all th' others. Ye niver see an Englishman that had anny judgment in lyin'. Th' corryspondint iv th' Daily Pail is out iv his class. He's carryin' lies to Lieville. How in th' wurruld can we compete with a counthry where ivry lab'rer's cottage projooces lies so delicate that th' workmen iv th' West can't undherstand thim?

We make our lies be machinery; they tur-rn out theirs be hand. They imitate th' best iv our canned lies to deceive people that likes that kind, but f'r artists they have lies that appeals to a more refined taste. Sure I'd like to live among thim an' find out th' kind iv bouncers they tell each other. They must be gr-rand. I on'y know their export lies now—th' surplus lies they can't use at home. An' th' kind they sind out ar-re betther thin our best. Our lies is no more thin a conthradiction iv th' thruth; their lies appeals to th' since iv honesty iv anny civilized man."

"They can't hurt us with their lies," said Mr. Hennessy of our Western civilization. "We have th' guns an' we'll bate thim yet."

"Yes," said Mr. Dooley, "an' 'twill be like a man who's had his house desthroyed be a cyclone gettin' up an' kickin' at th' air."

THE FUTURE OF CHINA

"Be th' time th' Chinese gets through with this here job o' theirs," said Mr. Dooley, "they'll know a thing or two about good manners an' Christyan idees."

"They need thim," said Mr. Hennessy.

"They do so," said Mr. Dooley. "An' they'll get thim. By an' by th' allied foorces will proceed to Peking. It may not be in ye'er life time or in mine, or in th' life time iv th' ministhers, Hinnissy. They ar-re in no hurry. Th' ministhers ar-re as comfortable as they can be on a dite iv polo ponies an' bamboo, an' they have exercise enough dodgin' cannon balls to have no fear iv indygisthion. They'se no need of haste. Th' allied foorces must take no step forward while wan ar-rmed foe survives. It was rayported last week that th' advance had begun, but on sindin' out scouts 'twas discovered that th' asphalt road to th' capital was not r-ready an' th' gallant sojer boys was afraid to risk their beecycles on a defictive pavement. Thin th' parlor cars ordhered be th' Rooshan admiral has not arrived an' wan iv th' Frinch gin'rals lost an omelette, or whatever 'tis they wear on their shouldhers, an' he won't budge till it can be replaced fr'm Pahrs. A sthrong corps iv miners an' sappers has gone ahead f'r to lo-cate good resthrants on th' line iv march, but th' weather is cloudy an' th' silk umbrellys haven't arrived, an' they'se supposed to be four hundhred millyon Chiny-men with pinwheels an' Roman candles blockin' th' way, so th' advance has been postponed indifinitely. Th' American foorces is r-ready f'r to start immejately, but they ar-re not there yet. Th' British gin'ral is waitin' f'r th' Victorya cross befure he does annything, an' th' Japanese an' th' Rooshan is dancin' up an' down sayin' 'Afther you, me boy.'"

"But afther awhile, whin th' frost is on th' pumpkin an' th' corn is in th' shock, whin th' roads has been repaired, an' ivry gin'ral's lookin' his best, an' in no danger iv a cold on th' chist, they'll prance away. An' whin they get to th' city iv Peking a fine cillybration is planned be th' mission'ries. I see th' programme in th' pa-aper: First day, 10 A.M., prayers be th' allied mission'ries; 1 P.M., massacree iv the impress an' rile fam'ly; sicond day, 10 A.M., scatthrin' iv remains iv former kings; 11 A.M., disecration iv graves gin'rally; 2 P.M., massacree iv all gin'rals an' coort officials; third day, 12 noon, burnin' iv Peking; foorth day, gran' pop'lar massacree an' division iv territ'ry, th' cillybration to close with a rough-an'-tumble fight among th' allies."

"'Twill be a gr-reat occasion, Hinnissy, an' be-dad I'd like to be there to see it. Ye can't go too sthrong again' th' Chinee. Me frind th' impror iv Germany put it right. 'Brave boys,' says he, 'ye ar-re goin' out now,' he says, 'f'r to carry th' light iv Christyanity,' he says, 'an' th' teachin's iv th' German Michael,' he says, 'to th' benighted haythen beyant,' he says. 'Me an' Mike is watchin' ye' he says, 'an' we ixpict ye to do ye'er duty,' he says. 'Through you,' he says, 'I propose to smash th' vile Chinee with me mailed fist,' he says. 'This is no six-ounce glove fight, but demands a lunch-hook done up in eight-inch armor plate,' he says. 'Whin ye get among th' Chinee,' he says, 'raymimber that ye ar-re the van guard iv Christyanity,' he says, 'an' stick ye'er baynet through ivry hated infidel ye see,' he says. 'Lave thim undherstand what our westhren civilization means,' he says, 'an' prod thim good an' hard,' he says. 'Open their heads with ye'er good German swords to Eu-ropyan culture an' refinement,' he says. 'Spare no man that wears a pigtail,' he says. 'An,' he says, 'me an' th' German Michael will smile on ye as ye kick th' linin' out iv th' dhragon an' plant on th' walls iv Peking th' banner,' he says, 'iv th' cross, an',' he says, 'th' double cross,' he says. 'An' if be chance ye shud pick up a little land be th' way, don't lave e'er a Frinchman or Rooshan take it fr'm ye, or ye'll feel me specyal delivery hand on th' back iv ye'er neck in a way that'll do ye no kind iv good. Hock German Michael,' he says, 'hock me gran'father, hoch th' penny postage fist,' he says, 'hock mesilf,' he says. An th' German impror wint back to his bedroom f'r to wurruk on th' book he's goin' to br-ring out nex' year to take th' place iv th' bible.

"He's th' boy f'r me money. Whin th' German throops takes their part in th' desthruction iv Peking they'll be none iv th' allied foorces 'll stick deeper or throw th' backbone iv th' impress' ol' father higher thin th' la-ads fr'm th' home iv th' sausage. I hope th' cillybration 'll occur on Chris'mas day. I'd like to hear th' sojers singin' 'Gawd r-rest ye, merry Chinnymen' as they punchered thim with a baynit."

"'Twill be a good thing," said Mr. Hennessy.

"It will that," said Mr. Dooley.

"'Twill civilize th' Chinnymen," said Mr. Hennessy.

"'Twill civilize thim stiff," said Mr. Dooley. "An' it may not be a bad thing f'r th' r-rest iv th' wurruld. Perhaps contack with th' Chinee may civlize th' Germans."

PLATFORM MAKING

"That sthrikes me as a gran' platform," said Mr. Hennessy. "I'm with it fr'm start to finish."

"Sure ye are," said Mr. Dooley, "an' so ye'd be if it begun: 'We denounce Terence Hinnissy iv th' Sixth Ward iv Chicago as a thraitor to his country, an inimy iv civilization, an' a poor thing.' Ye'd say: 'While there are wan or two things that might be omitted, th' platform as a whole is a statesmanlike docymint, an' wan that appeals to th' intelligince iv American manhood.' That's what ye'd say, an' that's what all th' likes iv ye'd say. An' whin iliction day comes 'round th' on'y question ye'll ast ye'ersilf is: 'Am I with Mack or am I with Billy Bryan?' An accordin'ly ye'll vote."

"'Tis always th' same way, an' all platforms is alike. I mind wanst whin I was an alter-nate to th' county con-vintion—'twas whin I was a power in pollytics an' th' on'y man that cud do annything with th' Bohemian vote—I was settin' here wan night with a pen an' a pot iv ink befure me, thryin' to compose th' platform f'r th' nex' day, f'r I was a lithry man in a way, d'ye mind, an' I knew th' la-ads'd want a few crimps put in th' raypublicans in a ginteel style, an' 'd be sure to call on me f'r to do it. Well, I'd got as far down as th' tariff an' was thryin' f'r to express me opinyon without swearin', whin who shud come in but Lafferty, that was sicrety iv McMahon, that was th' Main Guy in thim days, but aftherward thrun down on account iv him mixin' up between th' Rorkes an' th' Dorseys. Th' Main Guy Down Town said he wudden't have no throuble in th' ward, an' he declared McMahon out. McMahon had too much money annyhow. If he'd kept on, dollar bills'd have been extinct outside iv his house. But he was a sthrong man in thim days an' much liked."

"Anyhow, Lafferty, that was his sicrety, come in, an' says he: 'What are ye doin' there?' says he. 'Step soft,' says I; 'I am at wurruk,' I says. 'Ye shudden't do lithry wurruk on an empty stomach,' says he. 'I do nawthin' on an empty stomach but eat,' says I. 'I've had me supper,' I says. 'Go 'way,' says I, 'till I finish th' platform,' I says. 'What's th' platform?' says he. 'F'r th' county con-vintion,' says I.

"Well, sir, he set down on a chair, an' I thought th' man was goin' to die right there on the premises with laughter. 'Whin ye get through with ye'er barkin',' says I, 'I'll throuble ye to tell me what ye may be doin' it f'r,' I says. 'I see nawthin' amusin' here but ye'er prisince,' I says, 'an' that's not a divvle iv a lot funnier than a wooden leg,' I says, f'r I was mad. Afther awhile he come to, an' says he: 'Ye don't raally think,' says he, 'that ye'll get a chanct to spring that platform,' he says. 'I do,' says I. 'Why,' he says, 'the platform has been adopted,' he says. 'Whin?' says I. 'Befure ye were born,' says he. 'In th' reign iv Bildad th' first,' says he—he was a larned man, was Lafferty, though a dhrinkin' man. All sicreties iv pollyticians not in office is dhrinkin' men, Hinnissy. 'Ive got th' copy iv it here in me pocket,' he says. 'Th' boss give it to me to bring it up to date,' he says. 'They was no sthrike last year an' we've got to put a sthrike plank in th' platform or put th' president iv th' Lumber Shovers' union on th' county board, an',' he says, 'they ain't room,' he says.

"'Why,' says Lafferty, 'ye ought to know th' histhry iv platforms,' he says. An' he give it to me, an' I'll give it to ye. Years ago, Hinnissy, manny years ago, they was a race between th' dimmycrats an' th' raypublicans f'r to see which shud have a choice iv principles. Th' dimmycrats lost. I dinnaw why. Mebbe they stopped to take a dhrink. Annyhow, they lost. Th' raypublicans come up an' they choose th' 'we commind' principles, an' they was nawthin' left f'r the dimmycrats but th' 'we denounce an' deplores.' I dinnaw how it come about, but th' dimmycrats didn't like th' way th' thing shtud, an' so they fixed it up between thim that whichiver won at th' iliction shud commind an' congratulate, an' thim that lost shud denounce an' deplore. An' so it's been, on'y the dimmycrats has had so little chanct f'r to do annything but denounce an' deplore that they've almost lost th' use iv th' other wurruds.

"Mack sets back in Wash'nton an' writes a platform f'r th' comity on risolutions to compose th' week afther. He's got a good job—forty-nine ninety-two, sixty-six a month—an' 'tis up to him to feel good. 'I—I mean we,' he says, 'congratulate th' counthry on th' matchless statesmanship, on-shrinkin' courage, steady devotion to duty an' principle iv that gallant an' hon'rable leader, mesilf,' he says to his sicrety. 'Take that,' he says, 'an' elaborate it,' he says. 'Ye'll find a ditchnry on th' shelf near the dure,' he says, 'if ye don't think I've put what I give ye sthrong enough,' he says. 'I always was,' he says, 'too retirin' f'r me own good,' he says. 'Spin out th' r-rest,' he says, 'to make about six thousan' wurruds,' he says, 'but be sure don't write annything too hot about th' Boer war or th' Ph'lippeens or Chiny, or th' tariff, or th' goold question, or our relations with England, or th' civil sarvice,' he says. 'Tis a foolish man,' he says,'that throws a hunk iv coal fr'm his own window at th' dhriver iv a brick wagon,' he says."

"But with Billy Bryan 'tis diff'rent. He's out in Lincoln, Neebrasky, far fr'm home, an' he says to himsilf: 'Me throat is hoarse, an' I'll exercise me other fac'lties,' he says. 'I'll write a platform,' he says. An' he sets down to a typewriter, an' denounces an' deplores till th' hired man blows th' dinner horn. Whin he can denounce an' deplore no longer he views with alarm an' declares with indignation. An' he sinds it down to Kansas City, where th' cot beds come fr'm."

"Oh, ye're always pitchin' into some wan," said Mr. Hennessy. "I bet ye Willum Jennings Bryan niver see th' platform befure it wint in. He's too good a man."

"He is all iv that," said Mr. Dooley. "But ye bet he knows th' rale platform f'r him is: 'Look at th' bad breaks Mack's made,' an' Mack's platform is: 'Ye'd get worse if ye had Billy Bryan.' An' it depinds on whether most iv th' voters ar-re tired out or on'y a little tired who's ilicted. All excipt you, Hinnissy. Ye'll vote f'r Bryan?"

"I will," said Mr. Hennessy.

"Well," said Mr. Dooley, "d'ye know, I suspicted ye might."

THE YACHT RACES

"In th' ol' times whin I was a yachtsman—" began Mr. Dooley.

"Scowman," said Mr. Hennessy.

"Yachtsman," said Mr. Dooley. "Whin I was a yachtsman, all a man needed to race was a flat-bottomed boat, an umbrella, an' a long dhrink. In thim days 'twas 'Up with th' mainsail an' out with th' jib, an' Cap'n Jawn first to th' Lake View pumpin' station fr th' see-gars.' Now 'tis 'Ho, fr a yacht race. Lave us go an' see our lawyers.' 'Tis 'Haul away on th' writ iv ne exeat,' an' 'Let go th' peak capias.' 'Tis 'Pipe all hands to th' Supreme Coort.' 'Tis 'A life on th' boundin' docket an' a home on th' rowlin' calendar.' Befure we die, Sir Lipton'll come over here fr that Cup again an' we'll bate him be gettin' out an overnight injunction. What's th' use iv buildin' a boat that's lible to tip an' spill us all into th' wet? Turn th' matther over to th' firm iv Wiggins, Schultz, O'Mally, Eckstein, Wopoppski, Billotti, Gomez, Olson, an' McPherson, an' lave us have th' law on him."

"I don't suppose, Hinnissy, I ought to be gettin' off me little jokes on a seeryous matther like this. What's it all about, says ye? Well, ye see, 'tis this way. Wanst befure th' war some la-ad fr'm this counthry took a boat acrost th' Atlantic an' run it again an English boat an' iv coorse, he won, not bein' tied to th' dock, an' they give him a Cup. I don't know why they give him a cup, but they give him a cup. He brought it back here an' handed it to a yacht club, which is an assocyation, Hinnissy, iv mimbers iv th' Bar. He says: 'Ye keep that cup on ye'er mantle-piece an' if e'er an Englishman wants it, don't ye give it to him.' Afther awhile, an Englishman that ownded a boat come afther th' cup, an 'twas lave go altogether, an' th' las' man to th' line knows what he is. He's an Englishman, iv coorse. That was all r-right too. But th' time come whin th' lagal pro-fission took a hand in th' game. 'Look here,' says they. 'Ye've vilated nearly all th' statues iv th' State iv Noo Jarsey already,' they says, 'an' if ye ain't careful, ye'll be hauled up fr contimpt iv coort,' they says. So they took th' matther in hand an' dhrew up th' r-right pa-apers. 'State iv Noo York, county iv Cook, s. s. Know all men be these prisints. To all magisthrates an' polis officers, greetin.' In re Sir Lipton again th' Cup. Ordhered that if Sir Lipton shall secure said Cup fr'm aforesaid (which he won't) he must build a boat as follows: Wan hundherd an' twinty chest, fifty-four waist, hip an' side pockets, carryin' three hundherd an' sixty-three thousan' cubic feet iv canvas; th' basement iv th' boat to be papered in green with yellow flowered dado, open plumbin', steam heat throughout, th' tinant to pay fr all repairs. Be means iv this infernal machine, if enable to kill off th' rile fam'ly, he will attimpt to cross th' stormy Atlantic, an' if successful, will arrive at th' risidince iv th' party of th' first part, said John Doe. Wanst there, he will consult with mimbers iv th' Noo York Bar Association, who will lead him to a firm iv competent expert accountants, who will give him his time, which is two minyits measured be th' invarse ratio iv th' distance fr'm th' binnacle to th' cook-stove, an' fr'm th' cook-stove, east be north to th' bowspirit. He will thin take his foolish boat down th' bay, an' if he keeps his health, he can rayturn to th' grocery business, f'r he's a jolly good fellow which nobody can deny.'

"Ye can see this, Hinnissy, that yachtin' has become wan iv thl larned profissions. 'Tis that that got th' la-ad fr'm Boston into it. They's a jolly Jack Tar f'r ye. In dhrawin' up a lease or framin' a bond, no more gallant sailor rides th' waves thin hearty Jack Larsen iv th' Amalgamated Copper Yacht Club. 'What ho?' says he. 'If we're goin' to have a race,' he says, 'shiver me timbers if I don't look up th' law,' he says. So he become a yachtsman. 'But,' says th' Noo York la-ads, thim that has th' Cup on their mantel-piece, 'Ye can race on'y on two conditions.' 'What ar-re they?' says Larsen. 'Th' first is that ye become a mimber iv our club.' 'With pleasure,' says he. 'Ye can't,' says they. 'An' havin' complied with this first condition, ye must give us ye'er boat,' says they. 'We don't want it,' they says. 'Th' terms suit me entirely,' says Cap. Larsen. 'I'm a simple sailor man an' I'll give ye me boat undher th' following conditions,' he says. 'First, that ye won't take it; second, that ye'll paint me name on th' side iv it in red letters, three feet high; third, that ye'll inthra-jooce me to th' Prince iv Wales; foorth, that I'll sail it mesilf. Nawthin',' he says, 'wud give me gr-reater pleasure thin to have me handsome an' expinsive raft in th' hands iv men who I wud considher it an honor to know,' he says. 'An' so,' he says, 'I'll on'y ask ye to sign a bond an' lave a small security, say about five hundherd thousan' dollars, in me hands in case anny paint shud be knocked off me boat,' he says. 'Yachtin' is a gintleman's spoort,' he says, 'an' in dalin' with gintlemen,' he says, 'ye can't be too careful,' he says."

"What's Sir Lipton doin' all this time?" asked Mr. Hennessy.

"He's preparin' his bond, makin' his will, an' goin' through th' other lagal preliminaries iv th' race. He's built a boat too. Th' King of England was aboord iv her, an' he was near killed, be havin' a mast fall on him. Th' Lord knows how he escaped. A mass iv steel weighin' a hundherd thousan' ton fell on his Majesty an' bounced off. Sir Lipton felt pretty bad about it. He didn't mind losin' a mast or two, but he didn't want annywan to know he had th' king aboord. 'Twud hurt business. 'Boys,' says he to th' rayporthers, 'th' King's on me yacht. D'ye hear me? Th' King's on me yacht. But don't say annything about it. I don't want to have it known. Don't print it onless ye have to, an' thin put it in an inconspicuous place, like th' first page. He's here sure enough, boys. Th' mast just fell on his Majesty. It nearly kilt him. I'm not sure it didn't kill him. He remained perfectly cool throughout. So did I. I was almost cold. So did both iv us. But, mind not a wurrud iv this in th' pa-apers.' I don't know how th' rayporthers got hold iv it. But they're a pryin' lot."

"How did th' mast come to fall?" asked Mr. Hennessy, eagerly. "D'ye suppose Sir Lipton is wan iv us?"

"S-sh," said Mr. Dooley, adding, softly, "he was bor-rn in Limerick."

POLYGAMY

"How manny wives has this here man Roberts that's thryin' to break into Congress?" Mr. Dooley asked.

"I dinnaw," said Mr. Hennessy; "I nivver heerd iv him."

"I think it's three," said Mr. Dooley. "No wondher he needs wurruk an' is fightin' hard fr th' job. I'm with him too, be hivens. Not that I'm be taste or inclination a marryin' man, Hinnissy. They may get me to th' altar some day. Th' best iv us falls, like Cousin George, an' there ar-re designin' women in this very block that I have me own throubles in dodgin'. But anny time ye hear iv me bein' dhrawn fr'm th' quite miseries an' exclusive discomforts iv single life ye may know that they have caught me asleep an' chloroformed me. It's thrue. But fr thim that likes it, it's all r-right, an' if a man's done something in his youth that he has to do pinance fr an' th' stations iv th' cross ain't sthrong enough, lave him, says I, marry as manny women as he wants an' live with them an' die contint. Th' Mormons thinks they ar-re commanded be the Lord fr to marry all th' ineligeable Swede women. Now, I don't believe th' Lord iver commanded even a Mormon fr to do annything so foolish, an' if he did he wudden't lave th' command written on a pie-plate an' burrid out there at Nauvoo, in Hancock county, Illinye. Ye can bet on that, Hinnissy."

"But if anny wan believes 'twas done, I say, lave him believe it an' lave him clasp to his bosom as manny Olesons as 'll have him. Sure in th' prisint state iv th' mathrimonyal market, as Hogan calls it, whin he goes down to coort th' rich Widow O'Brien, th' la-ad that wants to engage in interprises iv that sort ought to have a frind in ivry wan but th' men that keeps imploymint agencies.

"But no. Th' minyit a Mormon thries to break into a pollytical job, a dillygation rises an' says they: 'What!' they says, 'permit this polluted monsther fr to invade th' chaste atmosphere,' they says, 'iv th' house iv riprisintatives,' they says. 'Permit him fr to parade his fam'ly down Pinnsylvanya Av'noo an' block thraffic,' they says. 'Permit him mebbe to set in th' chair wanst occupied be th' laminted Breckinridge,' they says. An' they proceed fr to hunt th' poor, crowded man. An' he takes a day off to kiss his wife fr'm house to house, an' holds a meetin' iv his childher to bid thim good-by an' r-runs to hide in a cave till th' dillygation raymimbers that they have husbands iv their own an' goes home to cook th' supper.

"A Mormon, Hinnissy, is a man that has th' bad taste an' th' rellijion to do what a good manny other men ar-re restrained fr'm doin' be conscientious scruples an' th' polis. I don't want anny wife; ye, Hinnissy, ar-re satisfied, not to say con-tint, with wan; another la-ad feels that he'd be lonesome without tin. 'Tis a matther iv disposition. If iver I got started th' Lord on'y knows where I'd bring up. I might be like me frind an' fellow-sultan, Hadji Mohammed. Hadji has wives to burn, an' wanst in awhile he bur-rns wan. He has a betther job thin Congressman."

"Th' best a congressman can get is foorth-class postmasther an' a look in at th' White House on visitin' day. But Hadji, th' pop'lar an' iloquent sultan iv Sulu an' Bazeen iv th' Ohio iv th' Passyfic, owns his own palace an' disthributes his own jobs. No man can hold th' office iv bow-sthringer iv our impeeryal domain without a certy-ficate fr'm Hadji. From th' highest office in th' land to th' lowest, fr'm th' chief pizener to th' throne, to th' humblest ixicutioner that puts a lady in a bag an' dumps her into th' lake in th' Nine Millionth Assimbly district they look to Hadji Mohammed f'r their places. He is th' High Guy, th' Main Thing. He's ivrybody. When he quits wurrk th' governmint is over f'r th' day. An' does annywan thry to interfere with Hadji? Does annywan say 'Hadji, ye'll have to abandon two or three hundherd iv ye 'er firesides. Ye ar-re livin' jus' inside th' left field fince iv our domain an' 'tis a rule iv th' game that we've taken ye into that no wan shall have more thin wan wife at a time that annywan knows iv. In' behalf iv th' comity iv th' Society f'r th' Supprission iv Poly-gamy, I request ye to discard Nora an' Eileen an' Mary Ann an' Sue an' Bimbi an' th' r-rest iv th' bunch, an' cleave on'y to Lucille. I judge be her looks that she's th' first Missus Haitch.'

"No, sir. If he did he'd reach th' ship that runs between our outlying wards without a hair to his head. Instead iv reproachin' Hadji with his domestic habits, wan iv th' envoys that ar-re imployed in carryin' messages fr'm th' prisidint to his fellow-citizens, proceeds to th' pretty little American village iv Sulu, where he finds Hadji settin' up on a high chair surrounded be wives. 'Tis a domestic scene that'd make Brigham Young think he was a bachelor. Hadji is smokin' a good seegar an' occasionally histin' a dhrink iv cider, an' wan iv th' ladies is playin' a guitar, an' another is singin' 'I want ye my Sulu,' an' another is makin' a tidy, an' three or four hundred more ar-re sewin' patches on th' pants iv th' Hadji kids. An' th' ambassadure he says: 'Mos' rile an' luminous citizen, here is a copy iv th' Annual Thanksgivin' pro-clamation,' he says. 'Tis addhressed to all th' hearty husbandmen iv our belovid counthry, manin' you among others,' he says. 'An' here,' he says, 'is th' revised constitution,' he says.

'Th' original wan,' he says, 'was intinded f'r ol' stick-in-th'-muds that wudden't know th' difference between a harem an' a hoe,' he says. 'This wan,' he says, 'is more suited f'r th' prisint gay an' expansive times,' he says. 'It permits a man to cleave to as manny wives,' he says, 'as his race, color, an' prevyous condition iv servitude will permit,' he says. 'Thank ye kindly,' says Hadji, 'I'll threasure these here papers as a vallyable meminto fr'm that far distant home iv mine which I have niver see,' he says. 'I'd inthrojooce ye to Mrs. Hadji wan by wan,' he says, 'but 'twud be betther,' he says, 'f'r to stand up here an' be prisinted to her as a whole,' he says, 'f'r,' he says, ''tis growing late an' I want ye to come up to th' house,' he says, 'an' pick a mission'ry with me,' he says. 'A Baptist,' he says, 'raised on th' farm,' he says. An' Hadji holds his job an' looks for'rard to th' day whin we'll have female suffrage an' he can cast th' solid vote iv Sulu for himsilf f'r prisident."

"Thin," said Mr. Hennessy, "ye'er frind Roberts ought to move to what-d'ye-call-th' place."

"That's what I'm thinkin'," said Mr. Dooley. "But 'tis too bad f'r him he was borrn at home."

PUBLIC FICKLENESS

Mr. Dooley put his paper aside and pushed his spectacles up on his forehead. "Well," he said, "I suppose, afther all, we're th' mos' lively nation in th' wurruld. It doesn't seem many months ago since ye, Hinnissy, was down at th' depot cheerin' th' departin' heroes——"

"I niver was," said Mr. Hennessey. "I stayed at home."

"Since ye was down cheerin' th' departin' heroes," Mr. Dooley continued, "an' thryin' to collect what they owed ye. Th' papers was full iv news iv th' war. Private Jawn Thomas Bozoom iv Woonsocket, a mimber iv th' gallant an' devoted Wan Hundhred an' Eighth Rhode Island, accidentally slipped on a orange peel while attimptin' to lave th' recruitin' office an' sustained manny con-tu-sions. He rayfused to be taken home an' insisted on jinin' his rig'mint at th' rayciption in th' fair groun's. Gallant Private Bozoom! That's th' stuff that American heroes ar-re made iv. Ye find thim at th' forge an' at th' plough, an' dhrivin' sthreet cars, an' ridin' in th' same. The favored few has th' chanst to face th' bullets iv th'inimy. 'Tis f'r these unknown pathrites to prove that a man can sarve his counthry at home as well as abroad. Private Bozoom will not be f'rgot be his fellow-counthrymen. A rayciption has been arranged f'r him at th' Woonsocket op'ry-house, an' 'tis said if he will accipt it, th' vote iv th' State iv Rhode Island'll be cast f'r him f'r prisidint. 'Tis at such times as this that we reflict that th' wurruld has wurruk f'r men to do, an' mere politicians mus' retire to th' rear."

"That was a few months ago. Where's Bozoom now? If iver ye go to Woonsocket, Hinnissy, which Gawd f'rbid, ye'll find him behind th' counther iv th' grocery store ladlin' out rutabaga turnips into a brown paper cornucopy an' glad to be alive. An' 'tis tin to wan, an' more thin that, that th' town humorist has named him th' orange-peel hero, an' he'll go to his grave with that name. Th' war is over an' th' state iv war exists. If ye saw a man fall fr'm th' top iv a tin-story buildin' 'twud startle ye, wanst. If it happened again, 'twud surprise ye. But if ye saw a man fall ivry fifteen minyits ye'd go home afther awhile f'r supper an' ye wuddent even mintion it to ye'er wife."

"I don't know how manny heroes they ar-re in th' Philippeens. Down there a man is ayether a sojer or a casualty. Bein' a casualty is no good. I cud say about a man: 'He was a hero in th' war with Spain,' but how can I say: 'Shake hands with Bill Grady, wan iv th' ladin' casualties iv our late war?' 'Twud be no more thin to say he was wan iv th' gallant men that voted f'r prisidint in 1896.'"

{Illustration}

"No, Hinnissy, people wants novelties in war. Th' war fashions iv 1898 is out iv style. They ar-re too full in th' waist an' too long in th' skirt. Th' style has changed. There ar-re fifty thousand backward men in th' fair isles iv th' Passyfic fightin' to free th' Philippeen fr'm himsilf an' becomin' a casualty in th' operation, but no one is charterin' ar-rmy hospital ships fr thim."

"No one is convartin' anny steam yachts fr thim. No wan is sindin' eighty tons iv plum puddin' to complete th' wurruk iv destruction. They ar-re in a war that'd make th' British throops in Africa think they were drillin' fr a prize banner. But'tis an onfashionable war.' 'Tis an ol' war made over fr'm garments formerly worn be heroes. Whin a man is out in th' counthry with wan newspaper an' has read th' authentic dispatches fr'm Ladysmith an' Harrismith an' Willumaldensmith an' Mysteriousbillysmith an' the meetin' iv th' czar iv Rooshia with th' Impror Willum an' th' fire in th' packin' house an' th' report iv th' canal thrustees an' th' fightin' news an' th' want ads, an' afther he has r-read thim over twinty times he looks at his watch an' says he, 'Holy smoke, 'tis two hours to thrain time an' I suppose I'll have to r-read th' news fr'm th' Philippeens.' War, be hivins, is so common that I believe if we was to take on a fight with all th' wurruld not more thin half th' popylation iv New England'd die iv hear-rt disease befure they got into th' cellars."

"Th' new style iv war is made in London an' all our set is simply stuck on it. Th' casualties in th' Philippeens can walk home, but is it possible that many thrue an' well-dhressed American can stand to see th' signs iv th' ancient British aristocracy taken care iv be their own gover'mint? 'What,' says Lady what's-her-name (her that was th' daughter iv wan iv our bravest an' best racontoors). 'What.' she says, 'will anny American woman residin' in London see men shot down,' she says, 'that has but recently played polo in our very sight,' she says, 'an' be brought home in mere thransports,' she says. 'Ladies,' she says, 'lave us equip a hospital ship,' she says. 'I thrust,' she says, 'that all iv us has been long enough fr'm home to f'rget our despicable domestic struggles,' she says, 'an' think on'y iv humanity,' she says. An' whin she opens up th' shop fr subscriptions ye'd think fr'm th' crowd that 'twas th' first night iv th' horse show. I don't know what Lem Stiggins iv Kansas, marked down in th' roll, Private in th' Twintieth Kansas, Severely, I don't know what Private Severely thinks iv it. An' I wuddent like to know till afther Thanks-givin'.'"

"Don't be blatherin'," said Mr. Hennessy. "Sure ye can't ixpict people to be inthrested f'river in a first performance."

"No," said Mr. Dooley, "but whin th' audjeence gives th' comp'ny an encore it ought at laste to pretind that it's not lavin' f'r th' other show."

KENTUCKY POLITICS

"If th' Presidint doesn't step in an' interfere," said Mr. Hennessy, "they'll be bloodshed in Kentucky."

"What business is it iv Mack's?" Mr. Dooley protested. "Th' war's in this counthry, man alive! If 'twas in Boolgahria or Chiny or on th' head waters iv th' Bozoon river in th' sooltynate iv—iv—I dinnaw what—thin'twud be th' jooty iv our gover'mint f'r to resolve that th' inthrests iv humanity an' civilization an' th' advancement iv th' human kind required that we shud step in an' put a head on wan or both iv th' parties. But they'se no reason now, me boy, f'r us to do annything, f'r these are our own people, an' 'tis wan iv their rights, undher th' martial law that's th' foundation iv our institutions, to bate each other to death whiniver an' whereiver they plaze. 'Twud be all r-right f'r the Impror Willum to come in an' take a hand, but Gawd help him if he did, or th' Prsidint iv th' Fr-rinch or th' Impror iv Chiny. 'Twud be all r-right f'r thim. An' though we might meet thim at th' dure an' hand thim wan f'r their impydince, we'd be in th' wrong. Twud be a good job f'r Aggynaldoo, too, if he cud find himsilf an' had th' time It must be clear to him be what news he hears whin th' other pigrim father, Sinitor Hoar, calls on him in th' three where he makes his home, that what Kentucky needs now is wan an' on'y wan stable govermint an' a little public peace. He might restore peace at home an' abroad be cuttin' in, but th' poor la-ad has other things to think iv. I'd like to see him. It must be near a year since he had a shave or a hair cut, barrin' ridges made be bullets as he cleared th' fences."

"It looks to me as though th' raypublican is wr-rong," said Mr. Hennessy, with the judicial manner of a man without prejudices.

"Iv coorse he's wrong," said Mr. Dooley. "He starts wrong. An' th' dimmycrats ar-re r-right. They're always r-right. Tis their position. Th' dimmycrats ar-re right an' the raypublicans has th' jobs. It all come up because our vinerated party, Hinnissy, ain't quick at th' count. Man an' boy I've taken an intherest in politics all me life, an' I find th' on'y way to win an iliction is to begin f'r to count th' minyit ye've completed th' preliminaries iv closin' th' polls an' killin' th' other judges an' clerks.

"Th' dimmycrats counted, but th' count come too late. Be th' time th' apparent an' hidjous majority iv th' raypublicans was rayjooced to nawthin' an' a good liberal, substantial, legal an' riotous dimmycratic majority put in its place be ordher iv th' coorts, th' commonwealth iv Kentucky an' Jack Chinn, th' raypublican has been so long in th'job an' has become so wedded to it that ye cuddent shake him out with a can iv joynt powdher. It seems to him that there niver was a time whin he wasn't gov'nor."

{Illustration}

"Th' dimmycrats get together an' call on that learned an' incorruptible joodishary that's done so much to ilivate the party into high office, an' whin th' dure iv th' saloon is locked they say 'Bill,' they say, 'we're bein' robbed iv our suffrage,' says they. 'Th' hated enimy has stolen th' ballot an' thrampled on th' r-rights iv th' citizens,' says they, 'in the southern part iv th' state faster thin we cud undo their hellish wurruk in our own counties,' they says. 'They now hol' th' jobs,' they say, 'an' if they stay in they'se no more chanst iv iver ilictin' a dimmycrat again thin there wud be iv ilictin' a raypublican if we got in,' they say. 'Do ye mix us up a replevy writ an' we'll go over an' haul th' chair fr'm undher thim,' they say."

"So th' judge passes out a replevy writ be vartue iv th' thrust that's been reposed in him be th' comity and gives it to Colonel Jack Chinn, wan iv th' leaders iv th' Kentucky bar, f'r to serve. An' Colonel Jack Chinn ar-rms himsilf as becomes a riprisintative iv a gr-reat coort goin' to sarve a sacred writ iv replevy on th' usurper to th' loftiest or wan iv th' loftiest jobs that th' people iv a gloryous state can donate to a citizen. He sthraps on three gatlin' guns, four revolvers, two swords, a rifle, a shot gun, a baseball bat, a hand grenade (to be used on'y in case iv thirst), a pair iv handcuffs, brass knuckles, a sandbag, a piece of lead pipe in a stockin', a rabbit's foot f'r luck, a stove lid an' a can iv dinnymite, an' with siveral iv his cillybrated knives behind his ears, in his hair, between his teeth, an' gleamin' fr'm his pockets, he sallies forth on his sacred mission, an' gives th' writ to a clerk to sarve, an' stays in town himsilf, where he successfully resists all charges iv th' bartinder. Th' clerk goes up to th' state house, where th' gov'nor is ixicutin' th' high thrust reposed in him be himsilf, behind breastworks an' guarded be some iv th' most desp'rate an' pathriotic ruffyans in th' state. 'What have ye there?' says his ixcillincy, with his hand on th' sthring iv a dinnymite gun. 'A writ fr'm th' coort bouncin' ye fr'm ye'er high office,' says th' clerk. 'As a law abidin' citizen,' says his ixcillincy, 'an' an official enthrusted be th' people iv this glad state with th' exicution iv th' statutes I bow to th' law,' he says. 'But,' he says, 'I'll be hanged if I'll bow to th' decree iv anny low browed pussillanimous dimmycratic coort,' he says, 'Sojers,' he says, 'seize this disturber iv th' peace an' stick him in th' cellar. Jawn,' he says, 'ar-rm ye'ersilf an' proceed to th' raypublican timple iv justice in Hogan's saloon an' have th' stanch an' upright Judge Blood prepare some good honest writs iv th' party iv Lincoln an' Grant,' he says. 'In th' manetime, as th' constitootion has lost its sights an' the cylinder don't revolve,' he says, 'I suspind it an' proclaim martial law,' he says. 'I want a law,' he says, 'that mesilf an' all other good citizens can rayspict,' he says. 'I want wan,' he says, 'that's been made undher me own personal supervision,' he says. 'Hand-made, copper distilled, wan hun-dherd an' tin proof martial law ought to be good enough for anny Kentuckyan,' he says. So th' next ye hear th' sojers ar-re chasin' th' coorts out iv th' state, th' legislature is meetin' in Duluth, Pinsacola, an' Bangor, Maine, an' a comity iv citizens consistin' iv some iv the best gun fighters iv th' state ar-re meetin' to decide how th' conthroversay can be decided without loss iv blood or jobs. While they're in session th' gov'nor is in contimpt iv coort, the coorts ar-re in contimpt iv th' gov'nor, an' if annybody but Tiddy Rosenfclt has anny other feelin' f'r ayether iv thim I haven't heerd him speak."

"They ought to fire out the raypublican," said Mr. Hennessy. "Sure 'tis comin' to a nice state iv affairs whin th' likes iv him can defy the coorts."

"Thrue f'r ye," said Mr. Dooley. "But I don't like th' looks iv it fr'm our side iv th' house. Whiniver a dimmycrat has to go to coort to win an iliction I get suspicious. They'se something wr-rong in Kentucky, Hinnissy. We were too slow. Th' inimy got th' first cheat."

YOUNG ORATORY

"They'se wan thing that this counthry ought to be thankful f'r," said Mr. Dooley, laying down his paper, "an' that is that we still have a lot iv young an' growin' orators f'r to lead us on."

"Who's been oratin' now?" Mr. Hennessy asked.

"Me young frind Sinitor Beveridge, th' child orator iv Fall Creek. This engagin' an' hopeful la-ad first made an impression with his eloquince at th' age iv wan whin he addhressed a meetin' iv th' Tippecanoe club on th' issues iv th' day. At th' age iv eight he was illicted to th' United States Sinit, rayjoocin' th' average age iv that body to ninety-three years. In th' sinit, bein' a modest child, he rayfused to speak f'r five minyits, but was fin'lly injooced f'r to make a few thousan' remarks on wan iv th' subjects now much discussed by orators whin th' dures ar-re closed an' th' fire escapes broken."

"His subject was th' Ph'lippeens, an' he said he'd just come fr'm there. 'I have cruised,' he says, 'f 'r two thousan' miles through th' Ar-rchey Pelago—that's a funny name—ivry minyit a surprise an' delight to those that see me,' he says. 'I see corn growin' on banana threes; I see th' gloryous heights iv Ding Dong that ar-re irradyatin'. civilization like quills upon th' fretful porcypine,' he says. 'I see rice, coffee, rolls, cocoanuts, choice seegars, oats, hay, hard and soft coal, an' Gen'ral Otis—an' there's a man that I rayspict,' he says. 'I see flowers bloomin' that was superyor to anny conservatory in Poolasky county,' he says. 'I see th' low and vicious inhabitants iv th' counthry soon, I thrust, to be me fellow-citizens, an' as I set there an' watched th' sea rollin' up its uncounted millyons iv feet iv blue wather, an' th' stars sparklin' like lamp-posts we pass in th' night, as I see th' mountains raisin' their snow-capped heads f'r to salute th' sun, while their feet extinded almost to th' place where I shtud; whin I see all th' glories iv that almost, I may say, thropical clime, an' thought what a good place this wud be f'r to ship base-burnin' parlor stoves, an' men's shirtings to th' accursed natives iv neighborin' Chiny, I says to mesilf, 'This is no mere man's wurruk. A Higher Power even than Mack, much as I rayspict him, is in this here job. We cannot pause, we cannot hesitate, we cannot delay, we cannot even stop! We must, in other wurruds, go on with a holy purpose in our hearts, th' flag over our heads an' th' inspired wurruds iv A. Jeremiah Beveridge in our ears,' he says. An' he set down."

"Well, sir,'twas a gr-reat speech. 'Twas a speech ye cud waltz to. Even younger men thin Sinitor Beveridge had niver made grander orations. Th' throuble is th' sinit is too common fr such magnificent sintimints; its too common and its too old. Th' young la-ad comes fr'm home, where's he's paralyzed th' Lithry Society an' th' Debatin' Club, an' he loads himsilf up with a speech an' he says to himsilf: 'Whin I begin peggin' ar-round a few iv these vilets I'll make Ol' Hoar look like confederate money,' an' th' pa-apers tell that th' Infant Demostheens iv Barry's Junction is about fr to revive th oratorical thraditions iv th' sinit an' th' fire department comes up fr a week, an' wets down th' capitol buildin'. Th' speech comes off, they ain't a dhry eye in th' House, an' th' pa-apers say: 'Where's ye'er Dan'l Webster an' ye'er Champ Clark, now?' An' th' young man goes away an' has his pitchers took on a kinetoscope. He has a nice time while it lasts, Hinnissy, but it don't las' long. It don't las' long. Th' la-ad has th' wind, but it's endurance that counts."

"Th' wise ol' boys with their long whiskers discusses him over th' sivin-up game, an' says wan iv thim: 'What ye think iv th' kid's speech?' "Twas a good speech,' says th' other. 'It carries me back to me own boyhood days. I made a speech just like that durin' th' Mexican War. Oh, thim days, thim days! I lead th' ace, Mike.' An' afther awhile th' Boy Demostheens larns that while he's polishin' off his ipigrams, an' ol' guy, that spinds all his time sleepin' on a bench, is polishin' him off. Th' man that sinds seeds to his constitooents lasts longer thin th' wan that sinds thim flowers iv iloquence, an' though th' hand iv Gawd may be in th' Ph'lippeen question, it hasn't interfered up to date in th' sergeant-at-arms question. An' whin th' young man sees this he says, 'sky,' whin he means 'sky' an' not 'th' jooled canopy iv hiven,' an' he says, 'Ph'lippeens,' an' not 'th' gloryous isles iv th' Passyfic,' an' bein' onto th' character iv his fellow-sinitors, he mintions nobody higher in their prisence thin th' steward iv th' capitol. An' he niver makes a speech but whin he wants to smoke, an' thin he moves that th' sinit go into executive session. Thin he's a rale sinitor. I've seen it manny's th' time—th' boy orator goin' into th' sinit, an' comin' out a deef mute. I've seen a man that made speeches that was set to music an' played be a silver cornet band in Ioway that hadn't been in Congress fr a month befure he wudden't speak above a whisper or more thin an inch fr'm ye'er ear."

"Do ye think Hiven sint us to th' Ph'lippeens?" Mr. Hennessy asked.

"I don't know," said Mr. Dooley, "th' divvle take thim."

PUBLIC GRATITUDE

"This man Dewey—," began Mr. Dooley.

"I thought he was ye'er cousin George," Mr. Hennessy interrupted.

"I thought he was," said Mr. Dooley, "but on lookin' closer at his features an' r-readin' what th' pa-apers says about him, I am convinced that I was wrong. Oh, he may be a sicond cousin iv me Aunt Judy. I'll not say he ain't. There was a poor lot, all iv them. But I have no close rilitives in this counthry. 'Tis a way I have of savin' a little money. I'm like th' good an' gr-rateful American people. Th' further ye stay away fr'm thim th' more they like ye. Sicond-cousin-iv-me Aunt-Judy-George made a mistake comin' home, or if he did come home he ought've invistigated his welcome and see that it wasn't mined. A man cud stand up all day an' lave Packy Mountjoy whale away at him, but th' affiction iv th' American people is always aimed thrue an' is invaryably fatal."

"Th' la-ad Dougherty was in to-day, an' he expressed th' feelin's iv this grateful raypublic. He says, says he, 'This fellow Dewey ain't what I thought he was,' he says. 'I thought he was a good, broad, lib'ral man, an' it turns out he's a cheap skate,' he says. 'We made too much fuss over him,' he says. 'To think,' he says, 'iv him takin' th' house we give him an' tur-rnin' it over to his wife,' he says. ''Tis scand'lous,' he says. 'How much did ye con-thribute?' says I. 'I didn't give annything,' he says 'The collector didn't come around, an' I'm glad now I hung on to me coin,' he says. 'Well,' says I, 'I apprechate ye'er feelin's,' I says. 'Ye agree with th' other subscribers,' I says. 'But I've med up me mind not to lave annywan talk to me about Dewey,' I says, 'unless,' I says, 'he subscribed th' maximum amount iv th' subscription,' I says, 'thirty-eight cints,' I says. 'So I'll thank ye to tip-toe out,' I says, 'befure I give ye a correct imitation iv Dewey an' Mountjoy at th' battle of Manila,' I says. An' he wint away."

"Th' throuble with Dewey is he was so long away he lost his undherstanding iv th' thrue feelin' iv th' American people. George r-read th' newspapers, an' he says to himself: 'Be hivins, they think well iv what I done. I guess I'll put a shirt in me thrunk an' go home, fr 'tis hot out here, an' ivrybody'll be glad fr to see me,' he says. An' he come along, an' New York was r-ready fr him. Th' business in neckties had been poor that summer, an' they was necessity fr pullin' it together, an' they give George a welcome an' invited his admirers fr'm th' counthry to come in an' buy something fr th' little wans at home. An' he r-rode up Fifth Avnoo between smilin' rows iv hotels an' dhrug stores, an' tin-dollar boxes an' fifty-cint seats an' he says to himsilf: 'Holy smoke, if Aggynaldoo cud on'y see me now.' An' he was proud an' happy, an' he says: 'Raypublics ar-re not always ongrateful.' An' they ain't. On'y whin they give ye much gratichood ye want to freeze some iv it, or it won't keep."

"'Tis unsafe f'r anny man alive to receive th' kind wurruds that ought to be said on'y iv th' dead. As long as George was a lithograph iv himsilf in a saloon window he was all r-right. Whin people saw he cud set in a city hall hack without flowers growin' in it an' they cud look at him without smoked glasses they begin to weaken in their devotion. 'Twud've been th' same, almost, if he'd married a Presbyteeryan an' hadn't deeded his house to his wife. 'Dewey don't look much like a hero,' says wan man. 'I shud say not,' says another. 'He looks like annybody else.' 'He ain't a hero,' says another. 'Why, annybody cud've done what he did. I got an eight-year-old boy, an' if he cudden't take a baseball club an' go in an' bate that Spanish fleet into junk in twinty minyits I'd call him Alger an' thrade him off f'r a bicycle,' he says. 'I guess that's r-right. They say he was a purty tough man befure he left Wash'n'ton.' 'Sure he was. Why, so-an'-so-an'-so-an'-so.' 'Ye don't tell me!' 'Is there annything in that story about his beatin' his poor ol' aunt an' her iliven childher out iv four dollars?' 'I guess that's straight. Ye can tell be th' looks iv him he's a mean man. I niver see a man with squintin' eyes an' white hair that wudden't rob a church!' 'He's a cow'rd, too. Why, he r-run away at th' battle iv Manila. Ivrybody knows it. I r-read what Joe What's-His-Name wrote—th' br-rave corryspondint. He says this feller was sick at his stummick an' retired befure th' Spanish fire. Why, what'd he have to fight but a lot iv ol' row-boats? A good swimmer with sharp teeth cud've bit his way through th' whole Spanish fleet. An' he r-run away. I tell ye, it makes me tired to think iv th' way we abused th' Spanyards not long ago. Why, say, they done a lot betther thin this fellow Dewey, with his forty or fifty men-iv-war an' this gran' nation, miles away, standin' shoulder to shoulder at his back. They niver tur-rned over their property to their wives.' 'Yes,' says wan man, 'Dewey was a cow'rd. Let's go an' stone his house.' 'No,' says the crowd, 'he might come out. Let's go down to th' v'riety show an' hiss his pitcher in th' kinetoscope.' Well!'"

"Well what?" demanded Mr. Hennessy.

"Well," Mr. Dooley continued, "I was on'y goin' to say, Hinnissy, that in spite iv me hathred iv George as a man—a marrid man—an' me contimpt f'r his qualities as a fighter, in spite iv th' chickens he has stole an' the notes he has forged an' th' homes he has rooned, if he was to come r-runnin' up Archey road, as he might, pursooed be ladies an' gintlemen an' th' palajeem iv our liberties peltin him with rotten eggs an' ol' cats, I'd open th' dure fr him, an' whin he come in I'd put me fut behind it an' I'd say to th' grateful people: 'Fellow-citizens,' I'd say, 'lave us,' I'd say. 'They'se another hero down in Halstead Sthreet that's been marrid. Go down an' shivaree him. An' you, me thrusted collagues iv th' press, disperse to ye'er homes,' I'd say. 'Th' keyholes is closed f'r th' night, I'd say. An' thin I'd bolt th' dure an' I'd say, 'George, take off ye'er coat an' pull up to th' fire. Here's a noggin' iv whisky near ye'er thumb an' a good seegar f'r ye to smoke. I'm no hero-worshiper. I'm too old. But I know a man whin I see wan, an' though we cudden't come out an' help ye whin th' subscription list wint wild, be sure we think as much iv ye as we did whin ye'er name was first mintioned be th' stanch an' faithful press. Set here, ol' la-ad, an' warrum ye'er toes by th' fire. Set here an' r-rest fr'm th' gratichood iv ye'er fellow-counthrymen, that, as Shakspere says, biteth like an asp an' stingeth like an adder. R-rest here, as ye might r-rest at th' hearth iv millyons iv people that cud give ye no house but their own!"

"I dinnaw about that," said Mr. Hennessy. "I like Dewey, but I think he oughtn't to've give away th' gift iv th' nation."

"Well," said Mr. Dooley, "if 'twas a crime f'r an American citizen to have his property in his wife's name they'd be close quarthers in th' pinitinchry."

MARRIAGE AND POLITICS

"I see," said Mr. Hennessy, "that wan iv thim New York joods says a man in pollytics oughtn't to be marrid."

"Oh, does he?" said Mr. Dooley.

"Well, 'tis little he knows about it. A man in pollytics has got to be marrid. If he ain't marrid where'll he go f'r another kind iv throuble? An' where'll he find people to support? An unmarrid man don't get along in pollytics because he don't need th' money. Whin he's in th' middle iv a prim'ry, with maybe twinty or thirty iv th' opposite party on top iv him, thinks he to himsilf: 'What's th' good iv fightin' f'r a job? They'se no wan depindant on me f'r support,' an' he surrinders. But a marrid man says: 'What'll happen to me wife an' twelve small childher if I don't win out here today?' an' he bites his way to th' top iv th' pile an' breaks open th' ballot box f'r home and fireside. That's th' thruth iv it, Hinnissy. Ye'll find all th' big jobs held be marrid men an' all th' timpry clerkships be bachelors."

"Th' reason th' New York jood thinks marrid men oughtn't to be in pollytics is because he thinks pollytics is spoort. An' so it is. But it ain't amachoor spoort, Hinnissy. They don't give ye a pewter mug with ye'er name on it f'r takin' a chanst on bein' kilt. 'Tis a profissional spoort, like playin' base-ball f'r a livin' or wheelin' a thruck. Ye niver see an amachoor at annything that was as good as a profissional. Th' best amachoor ball team is beat be a bad profissional team; a profissional boxer that thrains on bock beer an' Swiss cheese can lam the head off a goold medal amachoor champeen that's been atin' moldy bread an' dhrinkin' wather f'r six months, an' th' Dago that blows th' cornet on th' sthreet f'r what annywan 'll throw him can cut the figure eight around Dinnis Finn, that's been takin' lessons f'r twinty year. No, sir, pollytics ain't dhroppin' into tea, an' it ain't wurrukin' a scroll saw, or makin' a garden in a back yard. 'Tis gettin' up at six o'clock in th' mornin' an' r-rushin' off to wurruk, an' comin' home at night tired an' dusty. Double wages f'r overtime an' Sundahs."

"So a man's got to be marrid to do it well. He's got to have a wife at home to make him oncomfortable if he comes in dhrunk, he's got to have little prattlin' childher that he can't sind to th' Young Ladies' academy onless he stuffs a ballotbox properly, an' he's got to have a sthrong desire f'r to live in th' av'noo an' be seen dhrivin' downtown in an open carredge with his wife settin' beside him undher a r-red parasol. If he hasn't these things he won't succeed in pollytics—or packin' pork. Ye niver see a big man in pollytics that dhrank hard, did ye? Ye never will. An' that's because they're all marrid. Th' timptation's sthrong, but fear is sthronger."

"Th' most domestic men in th' wurruld ar-re politicians, an' they always marry early. An' that's th' sad part iv it, Hinnissy. A pollytician always marries above his own station. That's wan sign that he'll be a successful pollytician. Th' throuble is, th' good woman stays planted just where she was, an' he goes by like a fast thrain by a whistlin' station. D'ye mind O'Leary, him that's a retired capitalist now, him that was aldherman, an' dhrainage thrustee, an' state sinitor f'r wan term? Well, whin I first knew O'Leary he wurruked down on a railroad section tampin' th' thrack at wan-fifty a day. He was a sthrong, willin' young fellow, with a stiff right-hand punch an' a schamin' brain, an' anny wan cud see that he was intinded to go to th' fr-ront. Th' aristocracy iv th' camp was Mrs. Cassidy, th' widdy lady that kept th' boordin'-house. Aristocracy, Hinnissy, is like rale estate, a matther iv location. I'm aristocracy to th' poor O'Briens back in th' alley, th' brewery agent's aristocracy to me, his boss is aristocracy to him, an' so it goes, up to the czar of Rooshia. He's th' pick iv th' bunch, th' high man iv all, th' Pope not goin' in society. Well, Mrs. Cassidy was aristocracy to O'Leary. He niver see such a stylish woman as she was whin she turned out iv a Sundah afthernoon in her horse an' buggy. He'd think to himsilf, 'If I iver can win that I'm settled f'r life,' an' iv coorse he did. 'Twas a gran' weddin'; manny iv th' guests didn't show up at wurruk f'r weeks."

"O'Leary done well, an' she was a good wife to him. She made money an' kept him sthraight an' started him for constable. He won out, bein' a sthrong man. Thin she got him to r-run f'r aldher-man, an' ye shud've seen her th' night he was inaugurated! Be hivins, Hinnissy, she looked like a fire in a pawnshop, fair covered with dimons an' goold watches an' chains. She was cut out to be an aldherman's wife, and it was worth goin' miles to watch her leadin' th' gran' march at th' Ar-rchy Road Dimmycratic Fife an' Dhrum Corps ball."

"But there she stopped. A good woman an' a kind wan, she cudden't go th' distance. She had th' house an' th' childher to care f'r an' her eddy-cation was through with. They isn't much a woman can learn afther she begins to raise a fam'ly. But with O'Leary 'twas diffrent. I say 'twas diff'rent with O'Leary. Ye talk about ye'er colleges, Hinnissy, but pollytics is th' poor man's college. A la-ad without enough book larnin' to r-read a meal-ticket, if ye give him tin years iv polly-tical life, has th' air iv a statesman an' th' manner iv a jook, an' cud take anny job fr'm dalin' faro bank to r-runnin th' threasury iv th' United States. His business brings him up again' th' best men iv th' com-munity, an' their customs an' ways iv speakin' an' thinkin' an robbin' sticks to him. Th' good woman is at home all day. Th' on'y people she sees is th' childher an' th' neighbors. While th' good man in a swallow-tail coat is addhressin' th' Commercial club on what we shud do f'r to reform pollytics, she's discussin' th' price iv groceries with th' plumber's wife an' talkin' over th' back fince to the milkman. Thin O'Leary moves up on th' boolyvard. He knows he'll get along all r-right on th' boolyvard. Th' men'll say: 'They'se a good deal of rugged common sinse in that O'Leary. He may be a robber, but they's mighty little that escapes him.' But no wan speaks to Mrs. O'Leary. No wan asts her opinion about our foreign policy. She sets day in an' day out behind th' dhrawn curtains iv her three-story brownstone risidence prayin' that somewan'll come in an' see her, an if annywan comes she's frozen with fear. An' 'tis on'y whin she slips out to Ar-rchey r-road an' finds th' plumber's wife, an' sets in th' kitchen over a cup iv tay, that peace comes to her. By an' by they offer O'Leary th' nommynation f'r congress. He knows he's fit for it. He's sthronger thin th' young lawyer they have now. People'll listen to him in Wash'nton as they do in Chicago. He says: 'I'll take it.' An' thin he thinks iv th' wife an' they's no Wash'nton f'r him. His pollytical career is over. He wud niver have been constable if he hadn't marrid, but he might have been sinitor if he was a widower."

"Mrs. O'Leary was in to see th' Dargans th' other day. 'Ye mus' be very happy in ye'er gran' house, with Mr. O'Leary doin' so well,' says Mrs. Dargan. An' th' on'y answer th' foolish woman give was to break down an' weep on Mrs. Dargan's neck."

"Yet ye say a pollytician oughtn't to get marrid," said Mr. Hennessy.

"Up to a certain point," said Mr. Dooley, "he must be marrid. Afther that—well, I on'y say that, though pollytics is a gran' career f'r a man, 'tis a tough wan f'r his wife."

ALCOHOL AS FOOD

"If a man come into this saloon—" Mr. Hennessy was saying.

"This ain't no saloon," Mr. Dooley interrupted. "This is a resthrant."

"A what?" Mr. Hennessy exclaimed.

"A resthrant," said Mr. Dooley. "Ye don't know, Hinnissy, that liquor is food. It is though. Food—an' dhrink. That's what a doctor says in the pa-apers, an' another doctor wants th' gover'mint to sind tubs iv th' stuff down to th' Ph'lipeens. He says 'tis almost issintial that people shud dhrink in thim hot climates. Th' prespiration don't dhry on thim afther a hard pursoot iv Aggynaldoo an' th' capture iv Gin'ral Pantaloons de Garshy; they begin to think iv home an' mother sindin' down th' lawn-sprinkler to be filled with bock, an' they go off somewhere, an' not bein' able to dhry thimsilves with dhrink, they want to die. Th' disease is called nostalgia or home-sickness, or thirst."

"'What we want to do fr our sojer boys in th' Ph'lipeens besides killin' thim,' says th' ar-rmy surgeon, 'is make th' place more homelike,' he says. 'Manny iv our heroes hasn't had th' deleeryum thremens since we first planted th' stars an' sthripes,' he says, 'an' th' bay'nits among th' people,' he says. 'I wud be in favor iv havin' th' rigimints get their feet round wanst a week, at laste,' he says. 'Lave us,' he says, 'reform th' reg'lations,' he says, 'an' insthruct our sojers to keep their powdher dhry an' their whistles wet,' he says."

"Th' idee ought to take, Hinnissy, fr th' other doctor la-ad has discovered that liquor is food. 'A man,' says he, 'can live fr months on a little booze taken fr'm time to time,' he says 'They'se a gr-reat dale iv nourishment in it,' he says. An' I believe him, fr manny's th' man I know that don't think iv eatin' whin he can get a dhrink. I wondher if the time will iver come whin ye'll see a man sneakin' out iv th' fam'ly enthrance iv a lunch-room hurridly bitin' a clove! People may get so they'll carry a light dinner iv a pint iv rye down to their wurruk, an' a man'll tell ye he niver takes more thin a bottle iv beer fr breakfast. Th' cook'll give way to th' bartinder and th' doctor 'll ordher people fr to ate on'y at meals. Ye'll r-read in th' pa-apers that 'Anton Boozinski, while crazed with ham an' eggs thried to kill his wife an' childher.' On Pathrick's day ye'll see th' Dr. Tanner Anti-Food Fife an' Drum corpse out at th' head iv th' procession instead iv th' Father Macchews, an' they'll be places where a man can be took whin he gets th' monkeys fr'm immodhrate eatin'. Th' sojers 'll complain that th' liquor was unfit to dhrink an' they'll be inquiries to find out who sold embammin' flood to th' ar-rmy—Poor people 'll have simple meals—p'raps a bucket iv beer an' a little crame de mint, an' ye'll r-read in th' pa-apers about a family found starvin' on th' North side, with nawthin' to sustain life but wan small bottle iv gin, while th' head iv th' family, a man well known to the polis, spinds his wages in a low doggery or bakeshop fuddlin' his brains with custars pie. Th' r-rich 'll inthrajoose novelties. P'raps they'll top off a fine dinner with a little hasheesh or proosic acid. Th' time'll come whin ye'll see me in a white cap fryin' a cocktail over a cooksthove, while a nigger hollers to me: 'Dhraw a stack iv Scotch,' an' I holler back: 'On th' fire.' Ye will not."

{Illustration}

"That's what I thought," said Mr. Hennessy.

"No," said Mr. Dooley. "Whisky wudden't be so much iv a luxury if 'twas more iv a necissity. I don't believe 'tis a food, though whin me frind Schwartzmeister makes a cocktail all it needs is a few noodles to look like a biled dinner. No, whisky ain't food. I think betther iv it thin that. I wudden't insult it be placin' it on th' same low plane as a lobster salad. Father Kelly puts it r-right, and years go by without him lookin' on it even at Hallowe'en. 'Whisky,' says he, 'is called the divvle, because,' he says, ''tis wan iv the fallen angels,' he says. 'It has its place,' he says, 'but its place is not in a man's head,' says he. 'It ought to be th' reward iv action, not th' cause iv it,' he says. 'It's f'r th' end iv th' day, not th' beginnin',' he says. 'Hot whisky is good f'r a cold heart, an' no whisky's good f'r a hot head,' he says. 'Th' minyit a man relies on it f'r a crutch he loses th' use iv his legs. 'Tis a bad thing to stand on, a good thing to sleep on, a good thing to talk on, a bad thing to think on. If it's in th' head in th' mornin' it ought not to be in th' mouth at night. If it laughs in ye, dhrink; if it weeps, swear off. It makes some men talk like good women, an' some women talk like bad men. It is a livin' f'r orators an' th' death iv bookkeepers. It doesn't sustain life, but, whin taken hot with wather, a lump iv sugar, a piece iv lemon peel, and just th' dustin' iv a nutmeg-grater, it makes life sustainable."

"D'ye think ye-ersilf it sustains life?" asked Mr. Hennessy.

"It has sustained mine f'r many years," said Mr. Dooley.

HIGH FINANCE

"I think," said Mr. Dooley, "I'll go down to th' stock yards an' buy a dhrove iv Steel an' Wire stock."

"Where wud ye keep it?" asked the unsuspecting Hennessy.

"I'll put it out on th' vacant lot," said Mr. Dooley, "an' lave it grow fat by atin' ol' bur-rd cages an' tin cans. I'll milk it hard, an' whin 'tis dhry I'll dispose iv it to th' widdies an' orphans iv th' Sixth Ward that need household pets. Be hivins, if they give me half a chanst, I'll be as gr-reat a fi-nanceer as anny man in Wall sthreet.

"Th' reason I'm so confident iv th' value iv Steel an' Wire stock, Hinnissy, is they're goin' to hur-rl th' chairman iv th' comity into jail. That's what th' pa-apers calls a ray iv hope in th' clouds iv dipression that've covered th' market so long. 'Tis always a bull argymint. 'Snowplows common was up two pints this mornin' on th' rumor that th' prisidint was undher ar-rest.' 'They was a gr-reat bulge in Lobster preferred caused be th' report that instead iv declarin' a dividend iv three hundhred per cint. th' comp'ny was preparin' to imprison th' boord iv directors.' 'We sthrongly ricommind th' purchase iv Con and Founder. This comp'ny is in ixcillint condition since th' hangin' iv th' comity on reorganization.'"

"What's th' la-ad been doin', Hinnissy? He's been lettin' his frinds in on th' groun' flure—an' dhroppin' thim into th' cellar. Ye know Cassidy, over in th' Fifth, him that was in th' ligislachure? Well, sir, he was a gr-reat frind iv this man. They met down in Springfield whin th' la-ad had something he wanted to get through that wud protect th' widdies an' orphans iv th' counthry again their own avarice, an' he must've handed Cassidy a good argymint, fr Cassidy voted fr th' bill, though threatened with lynchin' be stockholders iv th' rival comp'ny. He come back here so covered with dimons that wan night whin he was standin' on th' rollin' mill dock, th' captain iv th' Eliza Brown mistook his shirt front fr th' bridge lights an' steered into a soap facthry on th' lee or gas-house shore."

"Th' man made a sthrong impression on Cassidy. 'Twas: 'As me frind Jawn says,' or 'I'll ask Jawn about that,' or 'I'm goin' downtown to-day to find out what Jawn advises.' He used to play a dollar on th' horses or sivin-up fr th' dhrinks, but afther he met Jawn he wanted me to put in a ticker, an' he wud set in here figurin' with a piece iv chalk on how high Wire'd go if hoopskirts come into fashion again. 'Give me a dhrop iv whisky,' he says, 'f'r I'm inthrested in Distillers,' he says, 'an' I'd like to give it a shove,' he says. 'How's Gas?' he says. 'A little weak, to-day,'" says I.

"'Twill be sthronger,' he says. 'If it ain't,' says I, 'I'll take out th' meter an' connect th' pipe with th' ventilator. I might as well bur-rn th' wind free as buy it,'" I says.

"A couple iv weeks ago he see Jawn an' they had a long talk about it. 'Cassidy,' says Jawn, 'ye've been a good frind iv mine,' he says, 'an' I'd do annything in the wurruld f'r ye, no matther what it cost ye,' he says. 'If ye need a little money to tide over th' har-rd times till th' ligislachure meets again buy'—an' he whispered in Cassidy's ear. 'But,' he says,'don't tell annywan. 'Tis a good thing, but I want to keep it bottled up,'" he says.

"Thin Jawn took th' thrain an' begun confidin' his secret to a few select frinds. He give it to th' conductor on th' thrain, an' th' porther, an' th' candy butcher; he handed it to a switchman that got on th' platform at South Bend, an' he stopped off at Detroit long enough to tell about it to the deepo' policeman. He had a sign painted with th' tip on it an' hung it out th' window, an' he found a man that carrid a thrombone in a band goin' over to Buffalo, an' he had him set th' good thing to music an' play it through th' thrain. Whin he got to New York he stopped at the Waldorf Asthoria, an' while th' barber was powdhrin' his face with groun' dimons Jawn tol' him to take th' money he was goin' to buy a policy ticket with an' get in on th' good thing. He tol' th' bootblack, th' waiter, th' man at th' news-stand, th' clerk behind th' desk, an' th' bartinder in his humble abode. He got up a stereopticon show with pitchers iv a widow-an-orphan befure an' afther wirin', an' he put an advertisement in all th' pa-apers tellin' how his stock wud make weak men sthrong. He had th' tip sarved hot in all th' resthrants in Wall sthreet, an' told it confidintially to an open-air meetin' in Madison Square. 'They'se nawthin,' he says, 'that does a tip so much good as to give it circulation,' he says. 'I think, be this time,' he says, 'all me frinds knows how to proceed, but—Great Hivins!' he says. 'What have I done? Whin all the poor people go to get th' stock they won't be anny f'r thim. I can not lave thim thus in th' lurch. Me reputation as a gintleman an' a fi-nanceer is at stake,' he says. 'Rather than see these brave people starvin' at th' dure f'r a morsel iv common or preferred, I'll—I'll sell thim me own stock,' he says. An' he done it. He done it, Hinnissy, with unfalthrin' courage an' a clear eye. He sold thim his stock, an' so's they might get what was left at a raysonable price, he wrote a confidintial note to th' pa-apers tellin' thim th' stock wasn't worth thirty cints a cord, an' now, be hivins, they're talkin' iv puttin' him in a common jail or pinitinchry preferred. Th' ingratichood iv man."

"But what about Cassidy?" Mr. Hennessy asked.

"Oh," said Mr. Dooley, "he was in here las' night. 'How's our old frind Jawn?' says I. He said nawthin'. 'Have ye seen ye'er collidge chum iv late?' says I. 'Don't mintion that ma-an's name,' says he. 'To think iv what I've done f'r him,' he says, 'an' him to throw me down,' he says. 'Did ye play th' tip?' says I. 'I did,' says he. 'How did ye come out?' says I. 'I haven't a cint lift but me renommynation f'r th' ligislachure,' says he. 'Well,' says I, 'Cassidy,' I says, 'ye've been up again what th' pa-apers call hawt finance,' I says. 'What th' divvle's that?' says he. 'Well,' says I, 'it ain't burglary, an' it ain't obtainin' money be false pretinses, an' it ain't manslaughter,' I says. 'It's what ye might call a judicious seliction fr'm th' best features iv thim ar-rts,' I says. 'T'was too sthrong f'r me,' he says. 'It was,' says I. 'Ye're about up to simple thransom climbin', Cassidy,' I says."

THE PARIS EXPOSITION

"If this r-rush iv people to th' Paris exposition keeps up," said Mr. Hennessy, "they won't be enough left here f'r to ilict a prisidint."

"They'll be enough left," said Mr. Dooley. "There always is. No wan has gone fr'm Arrchey r-road, where th' voters ar-re made. I've looked ar-round ivry mornin' expectin' to miss some familyar faces. I thought Dorgan, th' plumber, wud go sure, but he give it up at th' las' moment, an' will spind his summer on th' dhrainage canal. Th' baseball season 'll keep a good manny others back, an' a number iv riprisintative cit'zens who have stock or jobs in th' wire mills have decided that 'tis much betther to inthrust their savin's to John W. Gates thin to blow thim in again th' sthreets iv Cairo."

"But takin' it by an' large 'twill be a hard winter f'r th' r-rich. Manny iv thim will have money enough f'r to return, but they'll be much sufferin' among thim. I ixpict to have people dhroppin' in here nex' fall with subscription books f'r th' survivors iv th' Paris exhibition. Th' women down be th' rollin' mills 'll be sewin' flannels f'r th' disthressed millyonaires, an' whin th' childher kick about th' food ye'll say, Hinnissy, 'Just think iv th' poor wretches in th' Lake Shore dhrive an' thank Gawd f'r what ye have.' Th' mayor 'll open soup kitchens where th' unforchnit people can come an' get a hearty meal an' watch th' ticker, an' whin th' season grows hard, ye'll see pinched an' hungry plutocrats thrampin' th' sthreets with signs r-readin': 'Give us a cold bottle or we perish.' Perhaps th' polis 'll charge thim an' bust in their stovepipe hats, th' prisidint 'll sind th' ar-rmy here, a conspiracy 'll be discovered at th' club to blow up th' poorhouse, an' volunteers 'll be called on fr'm th' nickel bed houses to protect th' vested inthrests iv established poverty."

"'Twill be a chanst f'r us to get even, Hinnissy. I'm goin' to organize th' Return Visitin' Nurses' association, composed entirely iv victims iv th' parent plant. 'Twill be worth lookin' at to see th' ladies fr'm th' stock yards r-rushin' into some wretched home down in Peerary avenue, grabbin' th' misthress iv th' house be th' shouldhers an' makin' her change her onhealthy silk dhress f'r a pink wrapper, shovelin' in a little ashes to sprinkle on th' flure, breakin' th' furniture an' rollin' th' baby in th' coal box. What th' r-rich needs is intilligint attintion. 'Don't ate that oatmeal. Fry a nice piece iv r-round steak with onions, give th' baby th' bone to play with, an' sind Lucille Ernestine acrost th' railroad thrack f'r a nickel's worth iv beer. Thin ye'll be happy, me good woman.' Oh, 'twill be gran'. I won't give annything to people that come to th' dure. More harm is done be indiscriminate charity than anny wan knows, Hinnissy. Half th' bankers that'll come to ye-er kitchen nex' winter cud find plenty iv wurruk to do if they really wanted it. Dhrink an' idleness is th' curse iv th' class. If they come to me I'll sind thim to th' Paris Survivors' Mechanical Relief Association, an' they can go down an' set on a cake iv ice an' wait till th' man in charge finds thim a job managin' a diamond mine."

{Illustration}

Mr. Hennessy dismissed Mr. Dooley's fancy sketch with a grin and remarked: "These here expositions is a gran' thing f'r th' progress iv th' wurruld."

"Ye r-read that in th' pa-apers," said Mr. Dooley, "an' it isn't so. Put it down fr'm me, Hinnissy, that all expositions is a blind f'r th' hootchy-kootchy dance. They'll be some gr-reat exhibits at th' Paris fair. Th' man that has a machine that'll tur-rn out three hundhred thousan' toothpicks ivry minyit'll sind over his inthrestin' device, they'll be mountains iv infant food an' canned prunes, an' pickle casters, an' pants, an' boots, an' shoes an' paintin's. They'll be all th' wondhers iv modhern science. Ye can see how shirts ar-re made, an' what gives life to th' sody fountain. Th' man that makes th' glue that binds 'll be wearin' more medals thin an officer iv th' English ar-rmy or a cinchry bicycle rider, an' years afther whin ye see a box iv soap ye'll think iv th' manufacthrer standin' up befure a hundhred thousan' frinzied Fr-rinchmen in th' Boss du Boloney while th' prisidint iv th' Fr-rinch places a goold wreath on his fair brow an' says: 'In th' name iv th' ar-rts an' science, undher th' motto iv our people, "Libertinity, insanity, an' frugality," I crown ye th' champeen soapmaker iv th' wurruld. {Cheers.} Be ye'er magnificint invintion ye have dhrawn closer th' ties between Paris an' Goshen, Indyanny {frantic applause}, which I hope will niver be washed away. I wish ye much success as ye climb th' lather iv fame.' Th' invintor is thin dhrawn ar-roun' th' sthreets iv Paris in a chariot pulled be eight white horses amid cries iv 'Veev Higgins,' 'Abase Castile,' et cethra, fr'm th' populace. An' manny a heart beats proud in Goshen that night. That's th' way ye think iv it, but it happens diff'rent, Hinnissy. Th' soap king, th' prune king, an' th' porous plaster king fr'm here won't stir up anny tumult in Paris this year. Th' chances ar-re th' prisidint won't know they're there, an' no wan'll speak to thim but a cab dhriver, an' he'll say: 'Th' fare fr'm th' Changs All Easy to th' Roo de Roo is eighteen thousan' francs, but I'll take ye there f'r what ye have in ye-er pockets.'"

"The millyonaire that goes over there to see th' piled up riches iv th' wurruld in sausage-makin' 'll take a look ar-round him an' he'll say to th' first polisman he meets: 'Gossoon, this is a fine show an' I know yon palace is full to th' seams with chiny-ware an' washtubs, but wud ye be so kind, mong brav', as to p'int out with ye-er club th' partic'lar house where th' houris fr'm th' sultan's harem dances so well without the aid iv th' human feet?' I know how it was whin we had th' fair here. I had th' best intintions in th' wurruld to find out what I ought to have larned fr'm me frind Armour, how with th' aid iv Gawdgiven machinery ye can make a bedstead, a pianola, a dozen whisk-brooms, a barrel iv sour mash whisky, a suit iv clothes, a lamp chimbly, a wig, a can iv gunpowdher, a bah'rl iv nails, a prisidintial platform, an' a bur-rdcage out iv what remains iv th' cow—I was determined to probe into th' wondhers iv science, an' I started fair f'r th' machinery hall. Where did I bring up, says ye? In th' fr-ront seat iv a playhouse with me eye glued on a lady iv th' sultan's coort, near Brooklyn bridge, thryin' to twisht out iv hersilf."

"No, Hinnissy, they'll be manny things larned be Americans that goes to Paris, but they won't be about th' 'convarsion iv boots into food, or vicey varsa,' as Hogan says. An' that's r-right. If I wint over there 'tis little time I'd be spindin' thryin' to discover how th' wondhers iv mechanical janius are projooced that makes livin' so much more healthy an' oncomfortable. But whin I got to Paris I'd hire me a hack or a dhray painted r-red, an' I'd put me feet out th' sides an' I'd say to th' dhriver: 'Rivolutionist, pint ye-er horse's head to'rds th'home iv th' skirt dance, hit him smartly, an' go to sleep. I will see th' snow-plow show an' th' dentisthry wurruk in th' pa-apers. F'r th' prisint I'll devote me attintion to makin' a noise in th' sthreets an' studyin' human nature.'"

"Ye'd be a lively ol' buck over there," said Mr. Hennessy, admiringly. "'Tis a good thing ye can't go."

"It is so," said Mr. Dooley. "I'm glad I have no millyonaire rilitives to be depindent on me f'r support whin th' show's over."

CHRISTIAN JOURNALISM

"I see," said Mr. Dooley, "that th' la-ad out in Kansas that thried to r-run a paper like what th' Lord wud r-run if he had lived in Topeka, has thrun up th' job."

"Sure, I niver heerd iv him," said Mr. Hennessy.

"Well, 'twus this way with him," Mr. Dooley explained. "Ye see, he didn't like th' looks iv th' newspapers. He got tired iv r-readin' how many rows iv plaits Mrs. Potther Pammer had on th' las' dhress she bought, an' whether McGovern oughtn't to go into th' heavy-weight class an' fight Jeffries, an' he says, says th' la-ad, 'This is no right readin' f'r th' pure an' passionless youth iv Kansas,' he says. 'Give me,' he says, 'a chanst an' I'll projooce th' kind iv organ that'd be got out in hiven,' he says, 'price five cints a copy,' he says, 'f'r sale be all newsdealers; f'r advertisin' rates consult th' cashier,' he says. So a man in Topeka that had a newspaper, he says: 'I will not be behindhand,' he says, 'in histin' Kansas up fr'm its prisint low an' irrellijous position,' he says. 'I don't know how th' inhabitants iv th' place ye refer to is fixed,' he says, 'f'r newspapers,' he says, 'an' I niver heerd iv annybody fr'm Kansas home-stakin' there,' he says, 'but if ye'll attind to th' circulation iv thim parts,' he says, 'I'll see that th' paper is properly placed in th' hands iv th' vile an' wicked iv this earth, where,' he says, 'th' returns ar-re more quick,' he says."

"Well, th' la-ad wint at it, an' 'twas a fine paper he made. Hogan was in here th' other day with a copy iv it an' I r-read it. I haven't had such a lithry threat since I was a watchman on th' canal f'r a week with nawthin' to r-read but th' delinquent tax list an' the upper half iv a weather map. 'Twas gran'. Th' editor, it seems, Hinnissy, wint into th' editoryal rooms iv th' pa-aper an' he gathered th' force around him fr'm their reg'lar jobs in th' dhrug stores, an' says he, 'Gintlemen,' he says, 'tell me ye'er plans f'r to enoble this here Christyan publication f'r to-day!' he says. 'Well,' says th' horse rayporther, 'they's a couple iv rabbits goin' to sprint around th' thrack at th' fair groun's,' he says. I think 'twud be a good thing f'r rellijon if ye'd lind me tin that I might br-eak th' sin-thralled bookys that come down here fr'm Kansas City f'r to skin th' righteous,' he says. 'No,' says th' editor, he says, 'no horse racin' in this paper,' he says. ''Tis th' roonation iv th' young, an' ye can't beat it,' he says. 'An' you, fair-haired youth,' he says, 'what d'ye do that makes ye'er color so good an' ye'er eye so bright?' 'I,' says th' la-ad, 'am th' boy that writes th' fightin' dope,' he says. 'They'se a couple iv good wans on at th' op'ra house to-night, an' if his Spiklets don't tin-can 'tis like findin' money in an ol' coat that—' 'Fightin',' says th' editor, 'is a crool an' onchristyan spoort,' he says. 'Instead iv chroniclin' th' ruffyanism iv these misguided wretches that weigh in at th' ringside at 125 poun's, an' I see in a pa-aper I r-read in a barber shop th' other day that Spike's gone away back—what's that I'm sayin'? Niver mind. D'ye go down to th' home iv th' Rivrind Aloysius Augustus Morninbinch an'interview him on th' question iv man's co-operation with grace in conversion. Make a nice chatty article about it an' I'll give ye a copy iv wan iv me books.' 'I will,' says th' la-ad, 'if he don't swing on me,' he says. The editor thin addhressed th' staff. 'Gintlemen,' he says, 'I find that th' wurruk ye've been accustomed to doin',' he says, 'is calc'lated f'r to disthroy th' morality an' debase th' home life iv Topeka, not to mintion th' surroundin' methrolopuses iv Valencia, Wanamaker, Sugar Works, Paxico an' Snokomo,' he says. 'Th' newspaper, instead iv bein' a pow'rful agent f'r th' salvation iv mankind, has become something that they want to r-read,' he says. 'Ye can all go home,' he says. 'I'll stay here an' write th' paper mesilf,' he says. 'I'm th' best writer ar-round here, annyhow, an' I'll give thim something that'll prepare thim f'r death,' he says.

"An' he did, Hinnissy, he did. 'Twas a gran' paper. They was an article on sewerage an' wan on prayin' f'r rain, an' another on muni-cipal ownership iv gas tanks, an' wan to show that they niver was a good milker ownded be a pro-fane man. They was pomes, too, manny iv thim, an' fine wans: 'Th' Man with th' Shovel,' 'Th' Man with th' Pick, 'Th' Man with th' Cash-Raygisther,' 'Th' Man with th' Snow Plow,' 'Th' Man with th' Bell Punch,' 'Th' Man with th' Skate,' 'Th' Man with No Kick Comin'.' Fine pothry, th' editor askin' who pushed this here man's forehead back an' planed down his chin, who made him wear clothes that didn't fit him and got him a job raisin' egg-plant f'r th' monno-polists in Topeka at a dollar a day. A man in th' editor's position ought to know, but he didn't, so he ast in th'pomes. An' th' advertisin', Hinnissy! I'd be scandalized f'r to go back readin' th' common advertisin' in th' vile daily press about men's pantings, an' Doesannyoneknowwhere Icangeta biscuit, an' In th' spring a young man's fancy lightly turns to Pocohontas plug, not made be th' thrusts. Th' editor left thim sacrilegious advertisements f'r his venal contimp'raries. His was pious an' nice: 'Do ye'er smokin' in this wurruld. Th' Christyan Unity Five-Cint See-gar is made out iv th' finest grades iv excelsior iver projooced in Kansas!' 'Nebuchednezzar grass seed, f'r man an' beast.' 'A handful iv meal in a barrel an' a little ile in a curse. Swedenborgian bran fried in kerosene makes th' best breakfast dish in th' wurruld.' 'Twus nice to r-read. It made a man feel as if he was in church—asleep."

"How did th'pa-aper sthrike th' people?" says ye. "Oh, it sthruck thim good. Says th' Topeka man, skinnin' over th' gossip about Christyan citizenship an' th' toolchest iv pothry: 'Eliza, here's a good paper, a fine wan, fr ye an' th' childher. Sind Tommy down to th' corner an' get me a copy iv th' Polis Gazette.'"

"Ye see, Hinnissy, th' editor wint to th' wrong shop fr what Hogan calls his inspiration. Father Kelly was talkin' it over with me, an' says he: 'They ain't anny news in bein' good. Ye might write th' doin's iv all th' convents iv th' wurruld on th' back iv a postage stamp, an' have room to spare. Supposin' ye took out iv a newspaper all th' murdhers, an' suicides, an' divorces, an elopements, an' fires, an' disease, an' war, an' famine,' he says, 'ye wudden't have enough left to keep a man busy r-readin' while he rode ar-roun' th' block on th' lightnin' express. No,' he says, 'news is sin an' sin is news, an' I'm worth on'y a line beginnin': "Kelly, at the parish-house, April twinty-sicond, in th' fiftieth year iv his age," an' pay fr that, while Scanlan's bad boy is good fr a column anny time he goes dhrunk an' thries to kill a polisman. A rellijious newspaper? None iv thim fr me. I want to know what's goin' on among th' murdher an' burglary set. Did ye r-read it?' he says. 'I did,' says I. 'What did ye think iv it?' says he. 'I know,' says I, 'why more people don't go to church,' says I."

THE ADMIRAL'S CANDIDACY

"I see," said Mr. Hennessy, "that Dewey is a candydate f'r prisidint."

"Well, sir," said Mr. Dooley, "I hope to hiven he won't get it. No rilitive iv mine iver held a pollytical job barrin' mesilf. I was precint captain, an' wan iv th' best they was in thim days, if I do say so that shudden't. I was called Cap f'r manny years aftherward, an' I'd've joined th' Gr-rand Army iv th' Raypublic if it hadn't been f'r me poor feet. Manny iv me rilitives has been candydates, but they niver cud win out again th' r-rest iv th' fam'ly. 'Tis so with Cousin George. I'm again him. I've been a rayspictable saloon-keeper f'r forty years in this ward, an' I'll not have th' name dhragged into pollytics."

"Iv coorse, I don't blame Cousin George. I'm with him f'r annything else in th' gift iv th' people, fr'm a lovin'-cup to a house an' lot. He don't mean annything be it. Did ye iver see a sailor thryin' to ride a horse? 'Tis a comical sight. Th' reason a sailor thries to ride a horse is because he niver r-rode wan befure. If he knew annything about it he wouldn't do it. So be Cousin George. Afther he'd been over here awhile an' got so 'twas safe f'r him to go out without bein' torn to pieces f'r soovenirs or lynched be a mob, he took a look ar-round him an' says he to a polisman: 'What's th' governmint iv this counthry?' 'Tis a raypublic,' says th' polisman. 'What's th' main guy called?' says George. 'He's called prisidint,' says th' polisman. 'Is it a good job?' says Cousin George. ''Tis betther thin thravelin' beat,' says th' bull. 'What's th' la-ad's name that's holdin' it now?' says Cousin George. 'Mack,' says th' cop. 'Irish?' says George. 'Cross,' says th' elbow. 'Where fr'm?' says George. 'Ohio,' says the peeler. 'Where's that?' says George. 'I dinnaw,' says th' bull. An' they parted th' best iv frinds."

"'Well,'" says George to himsilf, "'I guess I'll have to go up an' have a look at this la-ad's place,' he says, 'an' if it looks good,' he says, 'p'raps I cud nail it,' he says. An' he goes up an' sees Mack dictatin' his Porther Rickyan policy to a kinetoscope, an' it looks like a nice employmint f'r a spry man, an' he goes back home an' sinds f'r a rayporther, an' says he: 'I always believe since I got home in dealin' frankly with th' press. I haven't seen manny papers since I've been at sea, but whin I was a boy me father used to take the Montpelier Paleejum. 'Twas r-run be a man be th' name iv Horse Clamback. He was quite a man whin sober. Ye've heerd iv him, no doubt. But what I ast ye up here f'r was to give ye a item that ye can write up in ye'er own way an' hand to th' r-rest iv th' boys. I'm goin' to be prisidint. I like th' looks iv the job an' nobody seems to care f'r it, an' I've got so blame tired since I left th' ship that if I don't have somethin' to do I'll go crazy,' he says. 'I wisht ye'd make a note iv it an' give it to th' other papers,' he says. 'Ar-re ye a raypublican or a dimmycrat?' says the rayporter. 'What's that?' says Cousin George. 'D'ye belong to th' raypublican or th' dimmycrat party?' 'What ar-re they like?' says Cousin George. 'Th' raypublicans ar-re in favor iv expansion.' 'Thin I'm a raypublican.' 'Th' dimmycrats ar-re in favor iv free thrade.' 'Thin I'm a dimmycrat.' 'Th' raypublicans ar-re f'r upholdin' th' goold standard.' 'So'm I. I'm a raypublican there.' 'An' they're opposed to an income tax.' 'On that,' says Cousin George, 'I'm a dimmycrat. I tell ye, put me down as a dimmycrat. Divvle th' bit I care. Just say I'm a dimmycrat with sthrong raypublican leanings. Put it this way: I'm a dimmycrat, be a point raypublican, dimmycrat. Anny sailor man'll undherstand that.' 'What'll I say ye'er platform is?' 'Platform?' 'Ye have to stand on a platform.' 'I do, do I? Well, I don't. I'll stand on no platform, an' I'll hang on no sthrap. What d'ye think th'prisidincy is—a throlley car? No, sir, whin ye peek in th' dure to sell ye'er paper ye'll see ye'er Uncle George settin' down comfortable with his legs crossed, thrippin' up annywan that thries to pass him. Go out now an' write ye'er little item, f'r 'tis late an' all hands ar-re piped to bed,' he says."

"An' there ye ar-re. Well, sir, 'tis a hard year Cousin George has in store f'r him. Th' first thing he knows he'll have to pay f'r havin' his pitchers in th' pa-aper. Thin he'll larn iv siv'ral prevyous convictions in Vermont. Thin he'll discover that they was no union label on th' goods he delivered at Manila. 'Twill be pointed out be careful observers that he was ilicted prisidint iv th' A. P. A. be th' Jesuits. Thin somewan'll dig up that story about his not feelin' anny too well th' mornin' iv th' fight, an' ye can imajine th' pitchers they'll print, an' th' jokes that'll be made, an' th' songs: 'Dewey Lost His Appetite at th' Battle iv Manila. Did McKinley Iver Lose His?' An' George'll wake up th' mornin' afther iliction an' he'll have a sore head an' a sorer heart, an' he'll find that th' on'y support he got was fr'm th' goold dimmycratic party, an' th' chances ar-re he caught cold fr'm goin' out without his shawl an' cudden't vote. He'll find that a man can be r-right an' be prisidint, but he can't be both at th' same time. An' he'll go down to breakfast an' issue Gin'ral Ordher Number Wan, 'To All Superyor Officers Commandin' Admirals iv th' United States navy at home or on foreign service: If anny man mintions an admiral f'r prisidint, hit him in th' eye an' charge same to me.' An' thin he'll go to his office an' prepare a plan f'r to capture Dublin, th' capital iv England, whin th' nex' war begins. An' he'll spind th' r-rest iv his life thryin' to live down th' time he was a candydate."

"Well, be hivins, I think if Dewey says he's a dimmycrat an' Joyce is with him, I'll give him a vote," said Mr. Hennessy. "It's no sin to be a candydate f'r prisidint."

"No," said Mr. Dooley. "Tis sometimes a misfortune an' sometimes a joke. But I hope ye won't vote f'r him. He might be ilicted if ye did. I'd like to raymimber him, an' it might be I cudden't if he got th' job. Who was the prisidint befure Mack? Oh, tubby sure!"

CUSTOMS OF KENTUCKY

"Well, sir," said Mr. Dooley, "'tis good to see that th' gloryous ol' commonwealth iv Kentucky is itsilf again."

"How's that?" asked Mr. Hennessy.

"F'r some time past," said Mr. Dooley, "they's been nawthin' doin' that'd make a meetin' iv th' Epworth League inthrestin'. Th' bystanders in Kentucky has been as safe as a journeyman highwayman in Chicago. Perfectly innocent an' unarmed men wint into th' state an' come out again without a bullethole in their backs. It looked f'r awhile as if th' life iv th' ordn'ry visitor was goin' to be as harmless in Kentucky as in Utah, th' home iv th' desthroyers iv American domestic life. I dinnaw why it was, whether it was th' influence iv our new citizens in Cubia an' th' Ph'lippeens or what it was, but annyhow th' on'y news that come out iv Kentucky was as peaceful, Hinnissy, as th' rayports iv a bloody battle in South Africa. But Kentucky, as Hogan says, was not dead but on'y sleepin'. Th' other day that gran' ol' state woke up through two iv its foremost rapid firin' citizens."

"They met be chanst in a hotel con-tagious to a bar. Colonel Derringer was settin' in a chair peacefully fixin' th' hammer iv his forty-four Colt gun, presinted to him be his constitooents on th' occasion iv his mim'rable speech on th' nicissity iv spreadin' th' civilization iv th' United States to th' ends iv th' wur-ruld. Surroundin' him was Major Bullseye, a well-known lawyer, cattle-raiser an' journalist iv Athens, Bulger County, whose desthruction iv Captain Cassius Glaucus Wiggins at th' meetin' iv' th' thrustees in th' Sicond Baptist Church excited so much comment among spoortin' men three or four years ago, Gin'ral Rangefinder iv Thebes, Colonel Chivvy iv Sparta, who whittled Major Lycurgus Gam iv Thermopylae down to th' wishbone at th' anti-polygamist meetin' las' June, an' other well-known gintlemen."

"Th' party was suddenly confronted be Major Lyddite iv Carthage an' a party iv frinds who were in town for th' purpose iv protectin' th' suffrage again' anny pollution but their own. Colonel Derringer an' Major Lyddite had been inimies f'r sivral months, iver since Major Lyddite in an attimpt to desthroy wan iv his fellow-citizens killed a cow belongin' to th' janial Colonel. Th' two gintlemen had sworn f'r to slay each other at sight or thirty days, an' all Kentucky society has been on what Hogan calls th' *quee veev* or look-out f'r another thrajeedy to be added to th' long list iv sim'lar ivints that marks th' histhry iv th' Dark an' Bloody Groun'—which is a name given to Kentucky be her affectionate sons."

{Illustration}

"Without a wur-rud or a bow both gintlemen dhrew on each other an' begun a deadly fusillade. That is, Hinnissy, they begun shootin' at th' bystanders. I'll tell ye what th' pa-apers said about it. Th' two antagonists was in perfect form an' well sustained th' reputation iv th' state f'r acc'rate workmanship. Colonel Derringer's first shot caught a boot an' shoe drummer fr'm Chicago square in th' back amid consid'rable applause. Major Lyddite tied th' scoor be nailin' a scrubwoman on th' top iv a ladder. Th' man at th' traps sprung a bell boy whom th' Colonel on'y winged, thus goin' back wan, but his second barrel brought down a book-canvasser fr'm New York, an' this bein' a Jew man sint him ahead three. Th' Major had an aisy wan f'r th' head waiter, nailin' him just as he jumped into a coal hole. Four all. Th' Colonel thried a difficult polisman, lamin' him. Thin th' Major turned his attintion to his own frinds, an' made three twos in succession. Th' Colonel was not so forch'nate. He caught Major Bullseye an' Captain Wiggins, but Gin'ral Rangefinder was safe behind a barber's pole an' Colonel Chivvy fluttered out iv range. Thus th' scoor was tin to six at th' conclusion iv th' day's spoort in favor iv Major Lyddite. Unforchnately th' gallant Major was onable f'r to reap th' reward iv his excellent marksmanship, f'r in a vain indeavor f'r a large scoor, he chased th' barber iv th' sicond chair into th' street, an' there slippin' on a banana peel, fell an' sustained injuries fr'm which he subsequently died. In him th' counthry loses a valu'ble an' acc'rate citizen, th' state a lile an' rapid firin' son, an' society a leadin' figure, his meat-market an' grocery bein' wan iv th' largest outside iv Minerva. Some idee iv th' acc'racy iv th' fire can be gained fr'm th' detailed scoor, as follows: Lyddite, three hearts, wan lung, wan kidney, five brains. Derringer, four hearts, two brains. This has seldom been excelled. Among th' minor casualties resultin' fr'm this painful but delightful soiree was th' followin': Erastus Haitch Muggins, kilt be jumpin' fr'm th' roof; Blank Cassidy, hide an' pelt salesman fr'm Chicago, burrid undher victims; Captain Epaminondas Lucius Quintus Cassius Marcellus Xerxes Cyrus Bangs of Hoganpolis, Hamilcar Township, Butseen County, died iv hear-rt disease whin his scoor was tied. Th' las' named was a prominent leader in society, a crack shot an' a gintleman iv th' ol' school without fear an' without reproach. His son succeeds to his lunch car. Th' others don't count."

"'Twas a gr-reat day f'r Kentucky, Hinnissy, an' it puts th' gran' ol' state two or three notches ahead iv anny sim'lar community in th' wur-ruld. Talk about th' Boer war an' th' campaign in th' Ph'lippeens! Whin Kentucky begins f'r to shoot up her fav'rite sons they'll be more blood spilled thin thim two play wars'd spill between now an' th' time whin Ladysmith's relieved fr th' las' time an' Agynaldoo is r-run up a three in th' outermost corner iv Hoar County, state iv Luzon. They'se rale shootin' in Kentucky, an' whin it begins ivrybody takes a hand. 'Tis th' on'y safe way. If ye thry to be an onlooker an' what they calls a non-combatant 'tis pretty sure ye'll be taken home to ye'er fam'ly lookin' like a cribbage-boord. So th' thing fr ye to do is to be wan iv th' shooters ye'ersilf, load up ye'er gun an' whale away fr th' honor iv ye'er counthry."

"'Tis a disgrace," said Mr. Hennessy. "Where were th' polis?"

"This was not th' place fr a polisman," said Mr. Dooley. "I suspict though, fr'm me knowledge iv th' kind iv man that uses firear-rms that if some wan'd had th' prisence iv mind to sing out 'They'se a man at th' bar that offers to buy dhrinks fr th' crowd,' they'd be less casu'lties fr'm bullets, though they might be enough people kilt in th' r-rush to even it up. But whin I read about these social affairs in Kentucky, I sometimes wish some spool cotton salesman fr'm Matsachoosets, who'd be sure to get kilt whin th' shootin' begun, wud go down there with a baseball bat an' begin tappin' th' gallant gintlemen on th' head befure breakfast an' in silf definse. I'll bet ye he'd have thim jumpin' through thransoms in less thin two minyits, fr ye can put this down as thrue fr'm wan that's seen manny a shootin', that a man, barrin' he's a polisman, on'y dhraws a gun whin he's dhrunk or afraid. Th' gun fighter, Hinnissy, tin to wan is a cow'rd."

"That's so," said Mr. Hennessy. "But it don't do to take anny chances on."

"No," said Mr. Dooley, "he might be dhrunk."

A SOCIETY SCANDAL

"Well, sir, I guess I'm not up on etiket," said Mr. Dooley.

"How's that?" demanded Mr. Hennessy.

"I've been readin' about Willum Waldorf Asthor," replied Mr. Dooley, "an' th' throuble he had with a la-ad that bummed his way into his party. Ye see, Hinnissy, Willum Waldorf Asthor give a party at his large an' commodjious house in London. That's where he lives—in London—though he r-runs a hotel in New York, where ye can see half th' state iv Ioway near anny night, they tell me. Well, he give this party on a gran' scale, an' bought gr-reat slathers iv food an' dhrink, an' invited th' neighbors an' the neighbors' childher. But wan man he wudden't have. He's goin' over th' list iv th' people that's to come, an' he says to his sicrety: 'Scratch that boy. Him an' me bump as we pass by.' He didn't want this fellow, ye see, Hinnissy. I don't know why. They was dissatisfaction between thim; annyhow, he says: 'Scratch him,' an' he was out iv it."

"Well, wan night, th' fellow was settin' down f'r a bite to eat with Lady O——, an' Lady S——, an' Lady G——, an' Lady Y——, an' other ladies that had lost their names, an' says wan iv thim, 'Cap,' she says, 'ar-re ye goin' to Asthor's doin's tonight?' she says. 'Not that I know iv,' says th' Cap. 'He hasn't sint me anny wurrud that I'm wanted,' he says. 'What differ does it make,' says th' lady. 'Write an invitation f'r ye'rsilf on ye'er cuff an' come along with us,' says she. 'I'll do it,' says the Cap, an' he sint f'r an automobile an' goes along.

"Well, ivrything was all r-right f'r awhile, an' th' Cap was assaultin' a knuckle iv ham an' a shell iv beer, whin Willum Waldorf Asthor comes up an' taps him on th' shoulder an' says: 'Duck.' 'What name?' says th' Cap. 'Asthor,' says Willum. 'Oh,' says th' Cap, 'ye're th' American gazabo that owns this hut,' he says. 'I am,' says Willum. 'I can't go,' says th' Cap. 'Ye didn't ask me here an' ye can't sind me away,' he says. 'Gossoon, another shell iv malt, an' dhraw it more slow,' he says. 'I am an English gintleman an' I know me rights,' he says. 'Dure or window,' says Willum. 'Take ye'er choice,' he says. 'If ye insist,' says th' Cap, 'I'll take th' dure,' he says, 'but ye don't know th' customs iv civilization,' he says; an' th' hired man just grazed him on th' dure sthep.

"Well, Willum Waldorf Asthor was that mad, he wint down to his pa-aper office, an' says he, 'I want to put in an item,' he says, an' he put it in. 'It is wished,' he says, 'to be apprihinded,' he says, 'be those desirous not to have been misinformed,' he says, 'concarnin' th' recent appearance iv Cap Sir Mills at me party,' he says, 'that 'twas not be me that said Cap Sir Mills come to be on th' site,' he says, 'but rather,' he says, 'through a desire on th' part iv Cap Sir Mills to butt into a party to which his invitation was lost about three hours befure 'twas written,' he says."

"Well, now, ye'd think that was all right, wudden't ye? Ye'd say Asthor acted mild whin he didn't take down his goold ice pick from th' wall an' bate th' Cap over th' head. Th' Cap, though a ganial soul, had no business there. 'Twas Willum Waldorf Asthor that paid f'r the ice cream an' rented th' chiny. But that's where ye'd be wrong, an' that's where I was wrong. Whin th' Prince iv Wales heerd iv it he was furyous. 'What,' he says, 'is an English gintleman goin' to be pegged out iv dures be a mere American be descent?' he says. 'A man,' he says, 'that hasn't an entail to his name,' he says. 'An American's home in London is an Englishman's castle,' he says. 'As th' late Earl iv Pitt said, th' furniture may go out iv it, th' constable may enther, th' mortgage may fall on th' rooned roof, but a thrue Englishman'll niver leave,' he says, 'while they'se food an' dhrink,' he says. 'Willum Waldorf Asthor has busted th' laws iv hospitality, an' made a monkey iv a lile subjick iv th' queen,' he says. 'Hinceforth,' he says, 'he's ast to no picnics iv th' Buckingham Palace Chowder Club,' he says. An' th' nex' day Willum Waldorf Asthor met him at th' races where he was puttin' down a bit iv money an' spoke to him, an' th' Prince iv Wales gave him wan in th' eye. He must've had something in his hand, f'r the pa-aper said he cut him. P'raps 'twas his scipter. An' now no wan'll speak to Willum Waldorf Asthor, an' he's not goin' to be a jook at all, an' he may have to come back here an' be nachurlized over again like a Bohamian. He's all broke up about it. He's gone to Germany to take a bath."

"Lord, help us," said Mr. Hennessy, "can't he get wan nearer home?"

"It seems not," said Mr. Dooley. "Mebbe the Prince iv Wales has had th' wather cut off. He has a big pull with th' people in th' city hall."

DOINGS OF ANARCHISTS

"Why should anny man want to kill a king?" said Mr. Dooley. "That's what I'd like to know. Little gredge have I again' anny monarch in th' deck. Live an' let live's me motto. Th' more ye have in this wurruld th' less ye have. Make in wan place, lose in another's th' rule, me boy. Little joy, little sorrow. Takin' it all an' all I'd rather be where I am thin on a throne, an' be th' look iv things I'll have me wish. 'Tis no aisy job bein' a king barrin' th' fact that ye don't have to marry th' woman iv ye'er choice but th' woman iv somebody else's. 'Tis like takin' a conthract an' havin' th' union furnish th' foreman an' th' mateeryal. Thin if th' wurruk ain't good a wild-eyed man fr'm Paterson, Noo Jarsey, laves his monkey an' his hand organ an' takes a shot at ye. Thank th' Lord I'm not so big that anny man can get comfort fr'm pumpin' a Winchester at me fr'm th' top iv a house."

"But if I was king ne'er an organ grinder'd get near enough me to take me life with a Hotchkiss gun. I'd be so far away fr'm the multitood, Hinnissy, that they cud on'y distinguish me rile features with a spy-glass. I'd have polismen at ivry tur-rn, an' I'd have me subjicks retire to th' cellar whin I took me walk. Divvle a bit wud you catch me splattherin' mesilf with morthar an' stickin' newspapers in a hole in a corner shtone to show future gin'rations th' progress iv crime in this cinchry. They'd lay their own corner-shtone fr all iv me. I'd communicate with th' pop'lace be means iv ginral ordhers, an' I'd make it a thing worth tellin' about to see th' face iv th' gr-reat an' good King Dooley."

"Kings is makin' thimsilves too common. Nowadays an arnychist dhrops into a lunch-room at th' railroad depot an' sees a man settin' on a stool atin' a quarther section iv a gooseb'ry pie an' dhrinkin' a glass iv buttermilk. 'D'ye know who that is?' says th' lunch-counter lady. 'I do not,' says th' arnychist, 'but be th' look iv him he ain't much.' 'That's th' king,' says th' lady. 'Th' king, is it,' says th' arnychist. 'Thin here's fr wan king less,' he says, an' 'tis all over. A king ought to be a king or he oughtn't. He don't need to be a good mixer. If he wants to hang on he must keep out iv range. 'Tis th' kings an' queens that thrusts so much in th' lilety iv their people that they live in summer resort hotels an' go out walkin' with a dog that's hurted. Th' on'y person that ought to be able to get near enough a rale king to kill him is a jook, or th' likes iv that. Th' idee iv a man from Noo Jarsey havin' th' chanst!"

"What on earth's to be done about thim arnychists?" Mr. Hennessy asked. "What ails thim annyhow? What do they want?"

"Th' Lord on'y knows," said Mr. Dooley.

"They don't want annything, that's what they want. They want peace on earth an' th' way they propose to get it is be murdhrin' ivry man that don't agree with thim. They think we all shud do as they please. They're down on th' polis foorce an' in favor iv th' pop'lace, an' whin they've kilt a king they call on th' polis to save thim fr'm th' mob. An' between you an' me, Hinnissy, ivry arnychist I've knowed, an' I've met manny in me time, an' quite, law-abidin' citizens they was, too, had th' makin' iv a thradeejan in him. If they was no newspapers they'd be few arnychists. They want to get their pitchers in th' pa-apers an' they can't do it be wheelin' bananas through th' sthreets or milkin' a cow, so they go out an' kill a king. I used to know a man be th' name iv Schmitt that was a cobbler be profession an' lived next dure but wan to me. He was th' dacintist man ye iver see. He kep' a canary bur-rd, an' his devotion to his wife was th' scandal iv th' neighborhood. But bless my soul, how he hated kings. He cudden't abide Cassidy afther he heerd he was a dayscinded fr'm th' kings iv Connock, though Cassidy was what ye call a prolotoorio or a talkin' workin'man. An' th' wan king he hated above all others was th' king iv Scholizwig-Holstein, which was th' barbarous counthry he come fr'm. He cud talk fairly dacint about other kings, but this wan—Ludwig was his name an' I seen his pitcher in th' pa-apers wanst—wud throw him into a fit. He blamed ivrything that happened to Ludwig. If they was a sthrike he charged it to Ludwig. If Schwartzmeister didn't pay him f'r half-solin' a pair iv Congress gaiters he used to wear in thim days, he tied a sthring arround his finger f'r to remind him that he had to kill Ludwig. 'What have ye again' th' king?' says I. 'He is an opprissor iv th' poor,' he says. 'So ar-re ye,' I says, 'or ye'd mend boots free.' 'He's explodin' th' prolotoorio,' he says. 'Sure,' says I, 'th' prolotoorio can explode thimsilves pretty well,' says I. 'He oughtn't to be allowed to live in luxury while others starve,' he says. 'An' wud ye be killin' a man f'r holdin' a nice job?' says I. 'What good wud it do ye?' says I. 'I'd be th' emancipator iv th' people,' says he. 'Ye'd have th' wurred on th' coffin lid,' says I. 'Why,' says he, 'think iv me, Schmitt, Owgoost Schmitt, stalkin' forth to avinge th' woes iv th' poor,' he says. 'Loodwig, th' cursed, goes by. I jumps fr'm behind a three an' society is freed fr'm th' monsther,' he says. 'Think iv th' glory iv it,' he says. 'Owgoost Schmitt, emancipator,' he says. 'I'll prove to Mary Ann that I'm a man,' he says. Mary Ann was his wife. Her maiden name was Riley. She heard him say it. 'Gus,' says she, 'if iver I hear iv ye shootin' e'er a king I'll lave ye,' she says."

"Well, sir, I thought he was jokin', but be hivins, wan day he disappeared, an' lo an' behold, two weeks afther I picks up a pa-aper an' r-reads that me brave Schmitt was took up be th' polis f'r thryin' to cop a monarch fr'm behind a three. I sint him a copy iv a pa-aper with his pitcher in it, but I don't know if iver he got it. He's over there now an' his wife is takin' in washin'."

"It's vanity that makes arnychists, Hinnissy—vanity an' th' habits kings has nowadays iv bein' as common as life insurance agents."

"I don't like kings," said Mr. Hennessy, "but I like arnychists less. They ought to be kilt off as fast as they're caught."

"They'll be that," said Mr. Dooley. "But killin' thim is like wringin' th' neck iv a mickrobe."

ANGLO-AMERICAN SPORTS

"Hinnissy, if iver we have war with what me frind Carl Schurz'd call th' Mother County, it'll not come fr'm anny Vinnyzwalan question. Ye can't get me excited over th' throbbin' debate on th' location iv th' Orynocoo River or whether th' miners that go to Alaska fr goold ar're buried be th' Canajeen or th' American authorities. Ye bet ye can't. But some day we'll be beat in a yacht r-race or done up at futball an' thin what Hogan call th' dogs iv war'll break out iv th' kennel an' divastate th' wurruld."

"Well," said Mr. Hennessy, complacently, "if we wait fr that we might as well disband our navy."

"I dinnaw about that," said Mr. Dooley, "I dinnaw abut that; afther ye left to investigate th' ir'n foundhries an' other pitcheresque roons iv this misguided counthry, I wint out to give a few raw rahs fr me fellow colleejens, who was attimptin' to dimonsthrate their supeeryority over th' effete scholars iv England at what I see be th' pa-apers is called th' Olympian games. Ye get to th' Olympian games be suffocation in a tunnel. Whin ye come to, ye pay four shillin's or a dollar in our degraded currency, an' stand in th' sun an' look at th' Prince iv Wales. Th' Prince iv Wales looks at ye, too, but he don't see ye."

"Me frind, th' American ambassadure was there, an' manny iv th' seats iv larnin' in th' gran' stand was occupied be th' flower iv our seminaries iv meditation or thought conservatories. I r-read it in th' pa-apers. At th' time I come in they was recitin' a pome fr'm th' Greek, to a thoughtful-lookin' young profissor wearin' th' star-spangled banner fr a necktie an' smokin' a cigareet. 'Now, boys,' says th' profissor, 'all together.' 'Rickety, co-ex, co-ex, hullabaloo, bozoo, bozoo, Harvard,' says th' lads. I was that proud iv me belovid counthry that I wanted to take off me hat there an' thin an' give th' colledge yell iv th' Ar-rchey road reform school. But I was resthrained be a frind iv mine that I met comin' over. He was fr'm Matsachoosetts, an' says he: 'Don't make a disturbance,' he says. 'We've got to create a fav'rable impression here,' he says, 'Th' English,' he says, 'niver shows enthusyasm,' he says. 'Tis regarded as unpolite,' he says. 'If ye yell,' he says, 'they'll think we want to win,' he says, 'an' we didn't come over here to win,' he says. 'Let us show thim,' he says, 'that we're gintlemen, be it iver so painful,' he says. An' I resthrained mesilf be puttin' me fist in me mouth."

{Illustration}

"They was an Englishman standin' behind me, Hinnissy, an' he was a model iv behaviour f'r all Americans intindin' to take up their homes in Cubia. Ye cudden't get this la-ad war-rmed up if ye built a fire undher him. He had an eye-glass pinned to his face an' he niver even smiled whin a young gintleman fr'm Harvard threw a sledge hammer wan mile, two inches. A fine la-ad, that Harvard man, but if throwin' th' hammer's spoort, thin th' rowlin' mills is th' athletic cintre iv our belovid counthry. Whin an Englishman jumped further thin another la-ad, me frind th' Ice-box, says he: 'H'yah, h'yah!' So whin an American la-ad lept up in th' air as though he'd been caught be th' anchor iv a baloon, I says: 'H'yah, h'yah!' too. Whin a sign iv th' effete aristocracy iv England done up sivral free-bor-rn Americans fr'm Boston in a fut r-race, me frind the Farthest North, he grabs his wan glass eye an' says he: 'Well r-run, Cambridge!' he says; 'Well r-run,' he says. An' 'Well r-run, whativer colledge ye're fr'm,' says I, whin wan iv our la-ads jumped over a fence ahead iv some eager but consarvative English scholars."

"Well, like a good game, it come three an' three. Three times had victhry perched upon our banner an' thrice—I see it in th' pa-aper—had th' flag iv th' mother counthry proclaimed that Englishmen can r-run. It was thryin' on me narves an' I wanted to yell whin th' tie was r-run off but th' man fr'm Matsachoosetts says: 'Contain ye'ersilf,' he says. 'Don't allow ye'er frinzied American spirit to get away with ye'er manners,' he says. 'Obsarve.' he says, 'th' ca'm with which our brother Anglo-Saxon views th' scene,' he says. 'Ah!' he says, 'they're off an' be th' jumpin' George Wash'nton, I bet ye that fellow fr'm West Newton'll make that red-headed, long-legged, bread-ballasted Englishman look like thirty cints. 'Hurroo,' he says. 'Go on, Harvard,' he says. 'Go on,' he says. 'Rah, rah, rah,' he says. 'Ate him up, chew him up,' he says. 'Harvard!' he says."

"I looked ar-round at th' ca'm dispassyonate Englishman. He dhropped his eye-glass so he cud see th' race an' he had his cane in th' air. 'Well r-run,' he says. 'Well r-run, Cambridge,' he says. 'Pull him down,' he says. 'Run over him,' he says. 'Thrip him up,' he says. 'They can't r-run,' he says, 'except whin they're Ph'lipinos behind thim,' he says. 'Well r-run,' he says, an' he welted th' man fr'm Matsachoosetts with his cane. 'Be careful what ye're doin' there,' says th' Anglo-Saxon. 'If it wasn't f'r th' 'liance I'd punch ye'er head off,' he says. 'An',' says th' ca'm Englishman, 'if it wasn't f'r our common hurtage,' he says, 'I'd make ye jump over th' gran' stand,' he says. 'Th' English always cud beat us r-runnin',' says the sage iv Matsachoosetts. 'Th' Americans start first an' finishes last,' says th' Englishman. An' I had to pull thim apart."

"Whether it is that our American colleejans spinds too much iv their lung power in provin' their devotion to what Hogan calls their Almy Matthers or not, I dinnaw, but annyhow, we had to dhrag th' riprisintative iv our branch iv th' Anglo-Saxon an' Boheemyan civilization in th' three-mile race fr'm undher two thousand iv our cousins or brothers-in-law that was ca'mly an' soberly, but hurridly an' noisily chargin' acrost th' thrack to cheer their own man."

"Me frind fr'm Matsachoosets was blue as we winded our way to th' sthrangulation railway an' started back f'r home. 'I'm sorry,' he says, 'to lose me timper,' he says, 'but,' he says, 'afther all th' pretinded affection iv these people f'r us,' he says, 'an' afther all we've done f'r thim in Alaska an'—an' ivrywhere,' he says, 'an' thim sellin' us coal whin they might've sold it to th' Spanyards if th' Spanyards'd had th' money,' he says, 'to see th' conduct iv that coarse an' brutal Englishman—' 'Th' wan that won th' r-race?' says I. 'Yes,' he says. 'No, I mean th' wan that lammed me with his cane,' he says. 'If it hadn't been,' he says, 'that we're united,' he says, 'be a common pathrimony,' he says, 'I'd've had his life,' he says. 'Ye wud so,' says I, 'an' ye're r-right,' I says. 'If all th' la-ads enthered into th' r-races with th' same spirit ye show now,' I says, 'th' English flag'd be dhroopin' fr'm th' staff, an' Cyrus Bodley iv Wadham, Mass.,'d be paintin' th' stars an' sthripes on th' Nelson monnymint,' I says. 'Whin we hated th' English,' I says, 'an' a yacht r-race was li'ble to end in a war message fr'm the prisidint, we used to bate thim,' I says. 'Now,' says I, 'whin we're afraid to injure their feelin's,' I says, 'an' whin we 'pologise befure we punch, they bate us,' I says. 'They're used to 'pologisin' with wan hand an' punchin' with th' other,' I says. 'Th' on'y way is th' way iv me cousin Mike,' I says. 'He was a gr-reat rassler an' whin he had a full Nelson on th' foolish man that wint again him, he used to say, 'Dear me, am I breakin' ye'er neck, I hope so.'"

"But th' Matsachoosetts man didn't see it that way. An' some time, I tell ye, Hinnissy, an' Englishman'll put th' shot wan fut further than wan iv our men th' Lord save us fr'm th' disgrace!—an' th' next day we'll invade Canada."

"We ought to do it, annyhow," said Mr. Hennessy stoutly.

"We wud," said Mr. Dooley, "if we were sure we cud lave it aftherwards."

VOICES FROM THE TOMB

"I don't think," said Mr. Dooley, "that me frind Willum Jennings Bryan is as good an orator as he was four years ago."

"He's th' grandest talker that's lived since Dan'l O'Connell," said Mr. Hennessy.

"Ye've heerd thim all an' ye know," said Mr. Dooley. "But I tell ye he's gone back. D'ye mind th' time we wint down to th' Coleesyum an' he come out in a black alapaca coat an' pushed into th' air th' finest wurruds ye iver heerd spoke in all ye'er bor-rn days? 'Twas a balloon ascinsion an' th' las' days iv Pompey an' a blast on th' canal all in wan. I had to hold on to me chair to keep fr'm goin' up in th' air, an' I mind that if it hadn't been fr a crack on th' head ye got fr'm a dillygate fr'm Westconsin ye'd 've been in th' hair iv Gin'ral Bragg. Dear me, will ye iver f'rget it, th' way he pumped it into th' pluthocrats? 'I tell ye here an' now,' he says, 'they'se as good business men in th' quite counthry graveyards iv Kansas as ye can find in the palathial lunch-counthers iv Wall street,' he says. 'Whin I see th' face iv that man who looks like a two-dollar pitcher iv Napolyeon at Saint Heleena,' he says, 'I say to mesilf, ye shall not—ye shall not'—what th' divvle is it ye shall not do, Hinnissy?"

"Ye shall not crucify mankind upon a crown iv thorns," said Mr. Hennessy.

"Right ye ar-re, I forgot," Mr. Dooley went on. "Well, thim were his own wurruds. He was young an' he wanted something an' he spoke up. He'd been a rayporther on a newspaper an' he'd rather be prisidint thin write anny longer fr th' pa-aper, an' he made th' whole iv th' piece out iv his own head.

"But nowadays he has tin wurruds fr Thomas Jefferson an' th' rest iv th' sage crop to wan fr himself. 'Fellow-dimmycrats,' he says, 'befure goin' anny farther, an' maybe farin' worse, I reluctantly accipt th' nommynation fr prisidint that I have caused ye to offer me,' he says, 'an' good luck to me,' he says. 'Seein' th' counthry in th' condition it is,' he says, 'I cannot rayfuse,' he says. 'I will now lave a subject that must be disagreeable to manny iv ye an' speak a few wurruds fr'm th' fathers iv th' party, iv whom there ar-re manny,' he says, 'though no shame to th' party, fr all iv that,' he says. 'Thomas Jefferson, th' sage iv Monticello, says: "Ye can't make a silk purse out iv a sow's ear," a remark that will at wanst recall th' sayin' iv Binjamin Franklin, th' sage iv Camden, that "th' fartherest way ar-round is th' shortest way acrost." Nawthin' cud be thruer thin that onliss it is th' ipygram iv Andhrew Jackson, th' sage iv Syr-acuse, that "a bur-rd in th' hand is worth two in th' bush." What gran' wurruds thim ar-re, an' how they must torture th' prisint leaders iv th' raypublican party. Sam'l Adams, th' sage iv Salem, says: "Laugh an' the wurruld laughs with ye," while Pathrick Hinnery, th' sage iv Jarsey City, puts it that "ye shud always bet aces befure th' dhraw." Turnin' farther back into histhry we find that Brian Boru, th' sage iv Munsther, said: "Cead mille failthé," an' Joolyus Caesar, th' sage iv Waukeesha, says, "Whin ye're in Rome, do th' Romans." Nebuchedneezar—there's a name fr ye—th' sage iv I-dinnaw-where, says: "Ye can't ate ye'er hay an' have it." Solomon, th' sage iv Sageville, said, "Whin a man's marrid his throubles begins," an' Adam, th' sage iv Eden, put it that "A snake in th' grass is worth two in th' boots." Ye'll see be this, me good an' thrue frinds, that th' voices fr'm th' tombs is united in wan gran' chorus fr th' ticket ye have nommynated. I will say no more, but on a future occasion, whin I've been down in southern Injyanny, I'll tell ye what th' sages an' fathers iv th' party in th' Ancient an' Hon'rable Association iv Mound-Builders had to say about th' prisint crisis.'"

"'Tisn't Bryan alone, Mack's th' same way. They're both ancesther worshippers, like th' Chinese, Hinnissy. An' what I'd like to know is what Thomas Jefferson knew about th' throubles iv ye an' me? Divvle a wurrud have I to say again' Thomas. He was a good man in his day, though I don't know that his battin' av'rage 'd be high again' th' pitchin' iv these times. I have a gr-reat rayspict fr the sages an' I believe in namin' sthreets an' public schools afther thim. But suppose Thomas Jefferson was to come back here now an' say to himsilf: 'They'se a good dimmycrat up in Ar-rchy road an' I think I'll dhrop in on him an' talk over th' issues iv th' day.' Well, maybe he cud r-ride his old gray mare up an' not be kilt be the throlley cars, an' maybe th' la-ads'd think he was crazy an' not murdher him fr his clothes. An' maybe they wudden't. But annyhow, suppose he got here, an' afther he'd fumbled ar-round at th' latch—fr they had sthrings on th' dure in thim days—I let him in. Well, whin I've injooced him to take a bowl iv red liquor—fr in his time th' dhrink was white—an' explained how th' seltzer comes out an' th' cash raygisther wurruks, an' wather is dhrawn fr'm th' fassit, an' gas is lighted fr'm th' burner, an' got him so he wud not bump his head again' th' ceilin' ivry time th' beer pump threw a fit—afther that we'd talk iv the pollytical situation."

"'How does it go?' says Thomas. 'Well,' says I, 'it looks as though Ioway was sure raypublican,' says I. 'Ioway?' says he. 'What's that?' says he. 'Ioway,' says I, 'is a state,' says I. 'I niver heerd iv it,' says he. 'Faith ye did not,' says I. 'But it's a state just th' same, an' full iv corn an' people,' I says. 'An' why is it raypublican?' says he. 'Because,' says I, 'th' people out there is fr holdin' th'

Ph'lippeens,' says I. 'What th' divvle ar-re th' Ph'lippeens?' says he. 'Is it a festival,' says he, 'or a dhrink?' he says. 'Faith, 'tis small wondher ye don't know,' says I, 'f'r 'tis mesilf was weak on it a year ago,' I says. 'Th' Ph'lippeens is an issue,' says I, 'an' islands,' says I, 'an' a public nuisance,' I says. 'But,' I says, 'befure we go anny further on this subject,' I says, 'd'ye know where Minnysota is, or Westconsin, or Utah, or Californya, or Texas, or Neebrasky?' says I. 'I do not,' says he. 'D'ye know that since ye'er death there has growed up on th' shore iv Lake Mitchigan a city that wud make Rome look like a whistlin' station—a city that has a popylation iv eight million people till th' census rayport comes out?' I says. 'I niver heerd iv it,' he says. 'D'ye know that I can cross th' ocean in six days, an' won't; that if annything doesn't happen in Chiny I can larn about it in twinty-four hours if I care to know; that if ye was in Wash'nton I cud call ye up be tillyphone an ye'er wire'd be busy?' I says. 'I do not,' says Thomas Jefferson. 'Thin,' says I, 'don't presume to advise me,' I says, 'that knows these things an' manny more,' I says. 'An' whin ye go back where ye come fr'm an' set down with th' rest iv th' sages to wondher whether a man cud possibly go fr'm Richmond to Boston in a week, tell thim,' I says, 'that in their day they r-run a corner grocery an' to-day,' says I, 'we're op'ratin' a sixteen-story department store an' puttin' in ivrything fr'm an electhric lightin' plant to a set iv false teeth,' I says. An' I hist him on his horse an' ask a polisman to show him th' way home."

"Be hivins, Hinnissy, I want me advice up-to-date, an' whin Mack an' Willum Jennings tells me what George Wash'nton an' Thomas Jefferson said, I says to thim: 'Gintlemen, they larned their thrade befure th' days iv open plumbin',' I says. 'Tell us what is wanted ye'ersilf or call in a journeyman who's wurrukin' card is dated this cinchry,' I says. 'An' I'm r-right too, Hinnissy.'"

"Well," said Mr. Hennessy, slowly, "those ol' la-ads was level-headed."

"Thrue f'r ye," said Mr. Dooley. "But undher th' new iliction laws ye can't vote th' cimitries."

The NEGRO PROBLEM

"What's goin' to happen to th' naygur?" asked Mr. Hennessy.

"Well," said Mr. Dooley, "he'll ayther have to go to th' north an' be a subjick race, or stay in th' south an' be an objick lesson. 'Tis a har-rd time he'll have, annyhow. I'm not sure that I'd not as lave be gently lynched in Mississippi as baten to death in New York. If I was a black man, I'd choose th' cotton belt in prifrince to th' belt on th' neck fr'm th' polisman's club. I wud so."

"I'm not so much throubled about th' naygur whin he lives among his opprissors as I am whin he falls into th' hands iv his liberators. Whin he's in th' south he can make up his mind to be lynched soon or late an' give his attintion to his other pleasures iv composin' rag-time music on a banjo, an' wurrukin' fr th' man that used to own him an' now on'y owes him his wages. But 'tis th' divvle's own hardship fr a coon to step out iv th' rooms iv th' S'ciety fr th' Brotherhood iv Ma-an where he's been r-readin' a pome on th' 'Future of th' Moke' an' be pursooed be a mob iv abolitionists till he's dhriven to seek polis protection, which, Hinnissy, is th' polite name fr fracture iv th' skull.

"I was fr sthrikin' off th' shackles iv th' slave, me la-ad. 'Twas thrue I didn't vote fr it, bein' that I heerd Stephen A. Douglas say 'twas onconstitootional, an' in thim days I wud go to th' flure with anny man fr th' constitootion. I'm still with it, but not sthrong. It's movin' too fast fr me. But no matther. Annyhow I was fr makin' th' black man free, an' though I shtud be th' south as a spoortin' proposition I was kind iv glad in me heart whin Gin'ral Ulyss S. Grant bate Gin'ral Lee an' th' rest iv th' Union officers captured Jeff Davis. I says to mesilf, 'Now,' I says,'th' coon'll have a chanst fr his life,' says I, 'an' in due time we may injye him,' I says.

"An' sure enough it looked good fr awhile, an' th' time come whin th' occas'nal dollar bill that wint acrost this bar on pay night wasn't good money onless it had th' name iv th' naygur on it. In thim days they was a young la-ad—a frind iv wan iv th' Donohue boys—that wint to th' public school up beyant, an' he was as bright a la-ad as ye'd want to see in a day's walk. Th' larnin' iv him wud sind Father Kelly back to his grammar. He cud spell to make a hare iv th' hedge schoolmasther, he was as quick at figures as th' iddycated pig they showed in th' tint las' week in Haley's vacant lot, and in joggerphy, asthronomy, algybbera, jommethry, chimisthry, physiojnomy, bassoophly an' fractions, I was often har-rd put mesilf to puzzle him. I heerd him gradyooate an' his composition was so fine very few cud make out what he meant.

"I met him on th' sthreet wan day afther he got out iv school. 'What ar-re ye goin' to do f'r ye'ersilf, Snowball,' says I—his name was Andhrew Jackson George Wash'n'ton Americus Caslateras Beresford Vanilla Hicks, but I called him 'Snowball,' him bein' as black as coal, d'ye see—I says to him: 'What ar-re ye goin' to do f'r ye'ersilf?' I says. 'I'm goin' to enther th' profission iv law,' he says, 'where be me acooman an' industhry I hope,' he says, 'f'r to rise to be a judge,' he says, 'a congrissman,' he says, 'a sinator,' he says, 'an' p'rhaps,' he says, 'a prisidint iv th' United States,' he says. 'Theyse nawthin to prevint,' he says. 'Divvle a thing,' says I. 'Whin we made ye free,' says I, 'we opened up all these opporchunities to ye,' says I. 'Go on,' says I, 'an' enjye th' wealth an' position conferred on ye be th' constitootion,' I says. 'On'y,' I says, 'don't be too free,' I says. 'Th' freedom iv th' likes iv ye is a good thing an' a little iv it goes a long way,' I says, 'an' if I ever hear iv ye bein' prisidint iv th' United States,' I says, 'I'll take me whitewashing' away fr'm ye'er father, ye excelsior hair, poached-egg eyed, projiny iv tar,' I says, f'r me Anglo-Saxon feelin' was sthrong in thim days.

"Well, I used to hear iv him afther that defindin' coons in th' polis coort, an' now an' thin bein' mintioned among th' scatthrin' in raypublican county convintions, an' thin he dhropped out iv sight. 'Twas years befure I see him again. Wan day I was walkin' up th' levee smokin' a good tin cint seegar whin a coon wearin' a suit iv clothes that looked like a stained glass window in th' house iv a Dutch brewer an' a pop bottle in th' fr-ront iv his shirt, steps up to me an' he says: 'How dy'e do, Mistah Dooley,' says he. 'Don't ye know me—Mistah Hicks?' he says. 'Snowball,' says I. 'Step inside this dureway,' says I, 'less Clancy, th' polisman on th' corner, takes me f'r an octoroon,' I says. 'What ar-re ye do-in'?' says I. 'How did ye enjye th' prisidincy?' says I. He laughed an' told me th' story iv his life. He wint to practisin' law an' found his on'y clients was coons, an' they had no assets but their vote at th' prim'ry. Besides a warrant f'r a moke was the same as a letther iv inthroduction to th' warden iv th' pinitinchry. Th' on'y thing left f'r th' lawyer to do was to move f'r a new thrile an' afther he'd got two or three he thought ol' things was th' best an' ye do well to lave bad enough alone. He got so sick iv chicken he cudden't live on his fees an' he quit th' law an' wint into journalism. He r-run 'Th' Colored Supplimint,' but it was a failure, th' taste iv th' public lanin' more to quadhroon publications, an' no man that owned a resthrant or theaytre or dhrygoods store'd put in an adver-tisemint f'r fear th' subscribers'd see it an' come ar-round. Thin he attimpted to go into pollytics, an' th' best he cud get was carryin' a bucket iv wather f'r a Lincoln Club. He thried to larn a thrade an' found th' on'y place a naygur can larn a thrade is in prison an' he can't wurruk at that without committin' burglary. He started to take up subscriptions f'r a sthrugglin' church an' found th' profission was overcrowded. 'Fin'ly,' says he, "twas up to me to be a porther in a saloon or go into th' on'y business,' he says, 'in which me race has a chanst,' he says. 'What's that?' says I. 'Craps,' says he. 'I've opened a palachal imporyium,' he says, 'where,' he says, "twud please me very much,' he says, 'me ol' abolitionist frind,' he says, 'if ye'd dhrop in some day,' he says, 'an' I'll roll th' sweet, white bones f'r ye,' he says. ''Tis th' hope iv me people,' he says. 'We have an even chanst at ivry other pursoot,' he says, 'but 'tis on'y in craps we have a shade th' best iv it,' he says."

"So there ye ar-re, Hinnissy. An' what's it goin' to come to, says ye? Faith, I don't know an' th' naygurs don't know, an' be hivins, I think if th' lady that wrote th' piece we used to see at th' Halsted Sthreet Opry House come back to earth, she wudden't know. I used to be all broke up about Uncle Tom, but cud I give him a job tindin' bar in this here liquor store? I freed th' slave, Hinnissy, but, faith, I think' twas like tur-rnin' him out iv a panthry into a cellar."

"Well, they got to take their chances," said Mr. Hennessy. "Ye can't do annything more f'r thim than make thim free."

"Ye can't," said Mr. Dooley; "on'y whin ye tell thim they're free they know we're on'y sthringin' thim."

The AMERICAN STAGE

"I've niver been much iv a hand f'r th' theaytre," said Mr. Dooley. "Whin I was a young man an' Crosby's Opry house was r-runnin' I used to go down wanst in a while an' see Jawn Dillon throwin' things around f'r th' amusemint iv th' popylace an' whin Shakespere was played I often had a seat in th' gal'ry, not because I liked th' actin', d'ye mind, but because I'd heerd me frind Hogan speak iv Shakespere. He was a good man, that Shakespere, but his pieces is full iv th' ol' gags that I heerd whin I was a boy. Th' throuble with me about goin' to plays is that no matther where I set I cud see some hired man in his shirt sleeves argyin' with wan iv his frinds about a dog fight while Romeo was makin' th' kind iv love ye wuddent want ye'er daughter to hear to Juliet in th' little bur-rd cage they calls a balcony. It must've been because I wanst knowed a man be th' name iv Gallagher that was a scene painter that I cud niver get mesilf to th' pint iv concedin' that th' mountains that other people agreed was manny miles in th' distance was in no danger iv bein' rubbed off th' map be th' coat-tails iv wan iv th' principal char-ackters. An' I always had me watch out to time th' moon whin' twas shoved acrost th' sky an' th' record breakin' iv day in th' robbers' cave where th' robbers don't dare f'r to shtep on the rock f'r fear they'll stave it in. If day iver broke on th' level th' way it does on th' stage 'twud tear th' bastin' threads out iv what Hogan calls th' firmymint. Hogan says I haven't got th' dhramatic delusion an' he must be r-right f'r ye can't make me believe that twenty years has elapsed whin I know that I've on'y had time to pass th' time iv day with th' bartinder nex' dure.

"Plays is upside down, Hinnissy, an' inside out. They begin with a full statement iv what's goin' to happen an' how it's goin' to come out an' thin ye're asked to forget what ye heerd an' be surprised be th' outcome. I always feel like goin' to th' office an' gettin' me money or me lithograph pass back afther th' first act.

"Th' way to write a play is f'r to take a book an' write it over hindend foremost. They're puttin' all books on th' stage nowadays. Fox's 'Book iv Martyrs' has been done into a three-act farce-comedy an'll be projooced be Delia Fox, th' author, nex' summer. Webster's 'Onabridge Ditchnry' will be brought out as a society dhrama with eight hundherd thousan' char-ackters. Th' 'Constitution iv th' United States' (a farce) be Willum McKinley is r-runnin' to packed houses with th' cillybrated thradeejan Aggynaldoo as th' villain. In th' sixteenth scene iv th' last act they'se a naygur lynchin'. James H. Wilson, th' author iv 'Silo an' Ensilage, a story f'r boys,' is dhramatizin' his cillybrated wurruk an' will follow it with a dhramatic version iv 'Sugar Beet Culture,' a farm play. 'Th' Familiar Lies iv Li Hung Chang' is expicted to do well in th' provinces an' Hostetter's Almanac has all dates filled, I undherstand th' bible'll be r-ready f'r th' stage undher th'direction iv Einstein an' Opperman befure th' first iv th' year. Some changes has been niciss'ry f'r to adapt it to stage purposes, I see be th' pa-apers. Th' authors has become convinced that Adam an' Eve must be carrid through th' whole play, so they have considerably lessened th' time between th' creation an' th' flood an' have made Adam an English nobleman with a shady past an' th' Divvle a Fr-rinch count in love with Eve. They're rescued be Noah, th' faithful boatman who has a comic naygur son."

"I see be th' pa-aper th' stage is goin' to th' dogs what with it's Sappho's an' th' like iv that," said Mr. Hennessy.

"Well, it isn't what it used to be," said Mr. Dooley, "in th' days whin 'twas th' purpose iv th' hero to save th' honest girl from the clutches iv th' villin in time to go out with him an' have a shell iv beer at th' Dutchman's downstairs. In th' plays nowadays th' hero is more iv a villain thin th' villain himsilf. He's th' sort iv a man that we used to heave pavin' shtones at whin he come out iv th' stage dure iv th' Halsted Sthreet Opry House. To be a hero ye've first got to be an Englishman, an' as if that wasn't bad enough ye've got to have committed as many crimes as th' late H. H. Holmes. If he'd been born in England he'd be a hero. Ye marry a woman who swears an' dhrinks an' bets on th' races an' ye quarrel with her. Th' r-rest iv th' play is made up iv hard cracks be all th' charack-ters at each others' morals. This is called repartee be th' learned, an' Hogan. Repartee is where I say: 'Ye stole a horse' an' ye say: 'But think iv ye'er wife!' In Ar-rchy r-road 'tis called disordherly conduct. They'se another play on where a man r-runs off with a woman that's no betther thin she ought to be. He bates her an' she marries a burglar. Another wan is about a lady that ates dinner with a German. He bites her an' she hits him with a cabbage. Thin they'se a play about an English gintleman iv th' old school who thries to make a girl write a letter f'r him an' if she don't he'll tell on her. He doesn't tell an' so he's rewarded with th' love iv th' heroine, an honest English girl out f'r th' money."

"Nobody's marrid in th' modhern play, Hinnissy, an' that's a good thing, too, f'r annywan that got marrid wud have th' worst iv it. In th' ol' times th' la-ads that announces what's goin' to happen in the first act, always promised ye a happy marredge in th' end an' as ivrybody's lookin' f'r a happy marredge, that held the aujeence. Now ye know that th' hero with th' wretched past is goin' to elope with th' dhrunken lady an' th' play is goin' to end with th' couples prettily divorced in th' centher iv th' stage. 'Tis called real life an' mebbe that's what it is, but f'r me I don't want to see real life on th' stage. I can see that anny day. What I want is f'r th' spotless gintleman to saw th' la-ad with th' cigareet into two-be-fours an' marry th' lady that doesn't dhrink much while th' aujeence is puttin' on their coats."

"Why don't they play Shakespere any more?" Mr. Hennessy asked.

"I undherstand," said Mr. Dooley, "that they're goin' to dhramatize Shakespere whin th' dhramatizer gets through with th' 'Report iv th' Cinsus Department f'r 1899-1900.'"

TROUBLES OF A CANDIDATE

"I wisht th' campaign was over," said Mr. Dooley.

"I wisht it'd begin," said Mr. Hennessy. "I niver knew annything so dead. They ain't been so much as a black eye give or took in th' ward an' its less thin two months to th' big day."

"'Twill liven up," said Mr. Dooley, "I begin to see signs iv th' good times comin' again. 'Twas on'y th' other day me frind Tiddy Rosenfelt opened th' battle mildly be insinuatin' that all dimmycrats was liars, horse thieves an' arnychists. 'Tis thrue he apologized fr that be explainin' that he didn't mean all dimmycrats but on'y those that wudden't vote fr Mack but I think he'll take th' copper off befure manny weeks. A ladin' dimmycratic rayformer has suggested that Mack though a good man fr an idjiot is surrounded be th' vilest scoundhrels iver seen in public life since th' days iv Joolyus Caesar. Th' Sicrety iv th' Threeasury has declared, that Mr. Bryan in sayin' that silver is not convartible be th' terms iv th' Slatthry bankin' law iv 1870, an' th' sicond clause iv th' threaty iv Gansville, has committed th' onpard'nable pollytical sin iv so consthructin' th' facts as to open up th' possibility iv wan not knowin' th' thrue position iv affairs, misundhersthandin' intirely. If he had him outside he'd call him a liar. Th' raypublicans have proved that Willum Jennings Bryan is a thraitor be th' letther written be Dr. Lem Stoggins, th' cillybrated antithought agytator iv Spooten Duyvil to Aggynaldoo in which he calls upon him to do nawthin' till he hears fr'm th' doc. Th' letther was sint through th' postal authorities an' as they have established no post-office in Aggynaldoo's hat they cudden't deliver it an' they opened it. Upon r-readin' th' letther Horace Plog iv White Horse, Minnesota, has wrote to Willum Jennings Bryan declarin' that if he (Plog) iver went to th' Ph'lippeens, which he wud've done but fr th' way th' oats was sproutin' in th' stack, an' had been hit with a bullet he'd ixpict th' Coroner to hold Bryan to th' gran' jury. This was followed be th' publication iv a letther fr'm Oscar L. Swub iv East Persepalis, Ohio, declarin' that his sister heerd a cousin iv th' man that wash'd buggies in a livery stable in Canton say Mack's hired man tol' him Mack'd be hanged befure he'd withdraw th' ar-rmy fr'm Cuba."

"Oh, I guess th' campaign is doin' as well as cud be ixpicted. I see be th' raypublican pa-apers that Andhrew Carnegie has come out fr Bryan an' has conthributed wan half iv his income or five hundhred millyon dollars to th' campaign fund. In th' dimmycratic pa-apers I r-read that Chairman Jim Jones has inthercipted a letther fr'm the Prince iv Wales to Mack congratulatin' him on his appintmint as gintleman-in-waitin' to th' queen. A dillygation iv Mormons has started fr'm dimmycratic headquarthers to thank Mack fr his manly stand in favor iv poly-gamy an' th' raypublican comity has undher consideration a letther fr'm long term criminals advisin' their colleagues at large to vote fr Willum Jennings Bryan, th' frind iv crime."

"In a few short weeks, Hinnissy, 'twill not be safe fr ayether iv the candydates to come out on th' fr-ront porch till th' waitin' dillygations has been searched be a polisman. 'Tis th' divvle's own time th' la-ads that r-runs fr th' prisidincy has since that ol' boy Burchard broke loose again' James G. Blaine. Sinitor Jones calls wan iv his thrusty hinchman to his side, an' says he: 'Mike, put on a pig-tail, an' a blue shirt an' take a dillygation iv Chinnymen out to Canton an' congratulate Mack on th' murdher iv mission'ries in China. An',' he says, 'ye might stop off at Cincinnati on th' way over an' arrange fr a McKinley an' Rosenfelt club to ilict th' British Consul its prisidint an' attack th' office iv th' German newspaper,' he says. Mark Hanna rings fr his sicrety an', says he: 'Have ye got off th' letther fr'm George Fred Willums advisin' Aggynaldoo to pizen th' wells?' 'Yes sir.' 'An' th' secret communication fr'm Bryan found on an arnychist at Pattherson askin' him to blow up th' White House?' 'It's in th' hands iv th' tyepwriter.' 'Thin call up an employmint agency an' have a dillygation iv Jesuites dhrop in at Lincoln, with a message fr'm th' pope proposin' to bur-rn all Protestant churches th' night befure iliction.'"

"I tell ye, Hinnissy, th' candydate is kept mov-in'. Whin he sees a dilly-gation pikin' up th' lawn he must be r-ready. He makes a flyin' leap fr th' chairman, seizes him by th' throat an' says: 'I thank ye fr th' kind sintimints ye have conveyed. I am, indeed, as ye have remarked, th' riprisintative iv th' party iv manhood, honor, courage, liberality an' American thraditions. Take that back to Jimmy Jones an' tell him to put it in his pipe an' smoke it.' With which he bounds into th' house an' locks the dure while th' baffled conspirators goes down to a costumer an' changes their disguise. If th' future prisidint hadn't been quick on th' dhraw he'd been committed to a policy iv sthranglin' all the girl babies at birth."

"No,'tis no aisy job bein' a candydate, an' 'twud be no easy job if th' game iv photographs was th' on'y wan th' candydates had to play. Willum Jennings Bryan is photygraphed smilin' back at his smilin' corn fields, in a pair iv blue overalls with a scythe in his hand borrid fr'm th' company that's playin' 'Th' Ol' Homestead,' at th' Lincoln Gran' Opry House. Th' nex' day Mack is seen mendin' a rustic chair with a monkey wrinch, Bryan has a pitcher took in th' act iv puttin' on a shirt marked with th' union label, an' they'se another photygraph iv Mack carryin' a scuttle iv coal up th' cellar stairs. An' did ye iver notice how much th' candydates looks alike, an' how much both iv thim looks like Lydia Pinkham? Thim wondherful boardhin'-house smiles that our gifted leaders wears, did ye iver see annythin' so entrancin'? Whin th' las' photygrapher has packed his ar-ms homeward I can see th' gr-reat men retirin' to their rooms an' lettin' their faces down f'r a few minyits befure puttin' thim up again in curl-pa-apers f'r th' nex' day display. Glory be, what a relief 'twill be f'r wan iv thim to raysume permanently th' savage or fam'ly breakfast face th' mornin' afther iliction! What a raylief 'twill be to no f'r sure that th' man at th' dure bell is on'y th' gas collector an' isn't loaded with a speech iv thanks in behalf iv th' Spanish Gover'mint! What a relief to snarl at wife an' frinds wanst more, to smoke a seegar with th' thrust magnate that owns th' cider facthry near th' station, to take ye'er nap in th' afthernoon undisthurbed be th' chirp iv th' snap-shot! 'Tis th' day afther iliction I'd like f'r to be a candydate, Hinnissy, no matther how it wint."

"An' what's become iv th' vice-prisidintial candydates?" Mr. Hennessy asked.

"Well," said Mr. Dooley, "Th' las' I heerd iv Adly, I didn't hear annythin', an' th' las' I heerd iv Tiddy he'd made application to th' naytional comity f'r th' use iv Mack as a soundin' board."

A BACHELOR'S LIFE

"It's always been a wondher to me," said Mr. Hennessy, "ye niver marrid."

"It's been a wondher to manny," Mr. Dooley replied haughtily. "Maybe if I'd been as aisy pleased as most—an' this is not sayin' annything again you an' ye'ers, Hinnisy, fr ye got much th' best iv it—I might be th' father iv happy childher an' have money in th' bank awaitin' th' day whin th' intherest on th' morgedge fell due. 'Tis not fr lack iv opportunities I'm here alone, I tell ye that me bucko, fr th' time was whin th' sound iv me feet'd brings more heads to th' windies iv Ar-rchey r-road thin'd bob up to see ye'er fun'ral go by. An' that's manny a wan."

"Ah, well," said Mr. Hennessy, "I was but jokin' ye." His tone mollified his friend, who went on: "To tell ye th' truth, Hinnissy, th' raison I niver got marrid was I niver cud pick a choice. I've th' makin' iv an ixcillint ol' Turk in me, to be sure, fr I look on all the sect as iligeable fr me hand an' I'm on'y resthrained fr'm r-rentin' Lincoln Park fr a home an' askin' thim all to clave on'y to me, be me nachral modesty an' th' laws iv th' State iv Illinye. 'Twas always so with me an' I think it is so with most men that dies bachelors. Be r-readin' th' pa-apers ye'd think a bachelor was a man bor-rn with a depraved an' parvarse hathred iv wan iv our most cherished institootions, an' anti-expansionist d'ye mind. But'tis no such thing. A bachelor's a man that wud extind his benificint rule over all th' female wurruld, fr'm th' snow-capped girls iv Alaska to th' sunny eileens iv th' Passyfic. A marrid man's a person with a limited affection—a protictionist an' anti-expansionist, a mugwump, be hivins. 'Tis th' bachelor that's keepin' alive th' rivrince fr th' sect.

"Whin I was a young man, ye cud search fr'm wan end iv th' town to th' other fr me akel with th' ladies. Ye niver see me in them days, but 'twas me had a rogue's eye an' a leg far beyant th' common r-run iv props. I cud dance with th' best iv thim, me voice was that sthrong 'twas impossible to hear annywan else whin I sung 'Th' Pretty Maid Milkin' th' Cow,' an' I was dhressed to kill on Sundahs. 'Twas thin I bought th' hat ye see me wear at th' picnic. 'Twas 'Good mornin', Misther Dooley, an' will ye come in an' have a cup iv tay,' an' 'How d'ye do Misther Dooley, I didn't see ye at mass this mornin',' an' 'Martin, me boy, dhrop in an' take a hand at forty-fives. Th' young ladies has been askin' me ar-re ye dead.' I was th' pop'lar idol, ye might say, an' manny's th' black look I got over th' shouldher at picnic an' wake. But I minded thim little. If a bull again me come fr'm th' pope himsilf in thim days whin me heart was high, I'd tuck it in me pocket an' say: 'I'll r-read it whin I get time.'"

"Well, I'd take one iv th' girls out in me horse an' buggy iv a Sundah an' I'd think she was th' finest in th' wurruld an' I'd be sayin' all kinds iv jokin' things to her about marredge licenses bein' marked down on account iv th' poor demand an' how th' parish priest was thinkin' iv bein' thransferred to a parish where th' folks was more kindly disposed to each other an' th' likes iv that, whin out iv th' corner iv me eye I'd see another girl go by, an' bless me if I cud keep th' lid iv me r-right eye still or hold me tongue fr'm such unfortchnit remark as: 'That there Molly Heaney's th' fine girl, th' fine, sthrappin' girl, don't ye think so?' Well, ye know, afther that I might as well be dhrivin' an ice wagon as a pleasure rig; more thin wanst I near lost th' tip iv me nose in th' jamb iv th' dure thryin' to give an affictshionate farewell. An' so it wint on, till I got th' repytation iv a flirt an' a philandhrer fr no raison at all, d'ye mind, but me widespread fondness. I like thim all, dark an' light, large an' small, young an' old, marrid an' single, widdied an' divorced, an' so I niver marrid annywan. But ye'll find me photygraft in some albums an' me bills in more thin wan livery stable."

"I think marrid men gets on th' best fr they have a home an' fam'ly to lave in th' mornin' an' a home an' fam'ly to go back to at night; that makes thim wurruk. Some men's domestic throubles dhrives thim to dhrink, others to labor. Ye r-read about a man becomin' a millyonaire an' ye think he done it be his own exertions whin 'tis much again little 'twas th' fear iv comin' home impty handed an' dislike iv stayin' ar-round th' house all day that made him rich. Misther Standard Ile takes in millyons in a year but he might be playin' dominoes in an injine house if it wasn't fr Mrs. Standard Ile. 'Tis th' thought iv that dear quiet lady at home, in her white cap with her ca'm motherly face, waitin' patiently fr him with a bell-punch that injooces him to put a shtick iv dinnymite in somebody else's ile well an' bury his securities whin th' assissor comes ar-round. Near ivry man's property ought to be in wife's name an' most iv it is.

"But with a bachelor 'tis diff'rent. Ye an' I ar-re settin' here together an' Clancy dhrops in. Clancy's wife's away an' he's out fr a good time an' he comes to me fr it. A bachelor's fr th' enjymint of his marrid frinds' vacations. Whin Clancy's wife's at home an' I go to see him he r-runs th' pail out in a valise, an' we take our criminal dhrink in th' woodshed. Well, th' three iv us sits here an' pass th' dhrink an' sing our songs iv glee till about ilivin o'clock; thin ye begin to look over ye'er shouldher ivry time ye hear a woman's voice an' fin'lly ye get up an' yawn an' dhrink ivrything on th' table an' gallop home. Clancy an' I raysume our argymint on th' Chinese sityation an' afterwards we carol together me singin' th' chune an' him doin' a razor edge tinor. Thin he tells me how much he cares f'r me an' proposes to rassle me an' weeps to think how bad he threats his wife an' begs me niver to marry, f'r a bachelor's life's th' on'y wan, an' 'tis past two o'clock whin I hook him on a frindly polisman an' sind him thrippin'—th' polisman—down th' sthreet. All r-right so far. But in th' mornin' another story. If Clancy gets home an' finds his wife's rayturned fr'm th' seaside or th' stock yards, or whereiver'tis she's spint her vacation, they'se no r-rest f'r him in th' mornin'. His head may sound in his ears like a automobill an' th' look iv an egg may make his knees thremble, but he's got to be off to th' blacksmith shop, an' hiven help his helper that mornin'. So Clancy's gettin' r-rich an' puttin' a coopoly on his house."

"But with me 'tis diff'rent. Whin Phibbius Apollo as Hogan calls th' sun, raises his head above th' gas house, I'm cuddled up in me couch an' Morpus, gawd iv sleep, has a sthrangle holt on me. Th' alarm clock begins to go off an' I've just sthrength enough to raise up an' fire it through th' window. Two hours afthward I have a gleam iv human intillygince an' hook me watch out fr'm undher th' pillow. 'It's eight o'clock,' says I. 'But is it eight in th' mornin' or eight in th' evenin'?' says I. 'Faith, I dinnaw, an' divvle a bit care I. Eight's on'y a number,' says I. 'It riprisints nawthin',' says I."

"They'se hours enough in th' day f'r a free man. I'll turr-n over an' sleep till eight-wan and thin I'll wake up refreshed,' I says. 'Tis ilivin o'clock whin me tired lids part f'r good an' Casey has been here to pay me eight dollars an' findin' me not up has gone away f'r another year."

"A marrid man gets th' money, Hinnissy, but a bachelor man gets th' sleep. Whin all me marrid frinds is off to wurruk pound in' th' ongrateful sand an' wheelin' th' rebellyous slag, in th' heat iv th' afthernoon, ye can see ye'er onfortchnit bachelor frind perambulatin' up an' down th' shady side iv th' sthreet, with an umbrelly over his head an' a wurrud iv cheer fr'm young an' old to enliven his loneliness."

"But th' childher?" asked Mr. Hennessy slyly.

"Childher!" said Mr. Dooley. "Sure I have th' finest fam'ly in th' city. Without scandal I'm th' father iv ivry child in Ar-rchey r-road fr'm end to end."

"An' none iv ye'er own," said Mr. Hennessy.

"I wish to hell, Hinnissy," said Mr. Dooley savagely, "ye'd not lean against that mirror, I don't want to have to tell ye again."

THE EDUCATION OF THE YOUNG

The troubled Mr. Hennessy had been telling Mr. Dooley about the difficulty of making a choice of schools for Packy Hennessy, who at the age of six was at the point where the family must decide his career.

"'Tis a big question," said Mr. Dooley, "an' wan that seems to be worryin' th' people more thin it used to whin ivry boy was designed fr th' priesthood, with a full undherstandin' be his parents that th' chances was in favor iv a brick yard. Nowadays they talk about th' edycation iv th' child befure they choose th' name. 'Tis: 'Th' kid talks in his sleep. 'Tis th' fine lawyer he'll make.' Or, 'Did ye notice him admirin' that photygraph? He'll be a gr-reat journalist.' Or, 'Look at him fishin' in Uncle Tim's watch pocket. We must thrain him fr a banker.' Or, 'I'm afraid he'll niver be sthrong enough to wurruk. He must go into th' church.' Befure he's baptized too, d'ye mind. 'Twill not be long befure th' time comes whin th' soggarth'll christen th' infant: 'Judge Pathrick Aloysius Hinnissy, iv th' Northern District iv Illinye,' or 'Profissor P. Aloysius Hinnissy, LL.D., S.T.D., P.G.N., iv th' faculty iv Nothre Dame.' Th' innocent child in his cradle, wondherin' what ails th' mist iv him an' where he got such funny lookin' parents fr'm, has thim to blame that brought him into th' wurruld if he dayvilops into a sicond story man befure he's twenty-wan an' is took up be th' polis. Why don't you lade Packy down to th' occylist an' have him fitted with a pair iv eyeglasses? Why don't ye put goloshes on him, give him a blue umbrelly an' call him a doctor at wanst an' be done with it?"

"To my mind, Hinnissy, we're wastin' too much time thinkin' iv th' future iv our young, an' thryin' to larn thim early what they oughtn't to know till they've growed up. We sind th' childher to school as if 'twas a summer garden where they go to be amused instead iv a pinitinchry where they're sint fr th' original sin. Whin I was a la-ad I was put at me ah-bee abs, th' first day I set fut in th' school behind th' hedge an' me head was sore inside an' out befure I wint home. Now th' first thing we larn th' future Mark Hannas an' Jawn D. Gateses iv our naytion is waltzin', singin', an' cuttin' pitchers out iv a book. We'd be much betther teachin' thim th' sthrangle hold, fr that's what they need in life."

"I know what'll happen. Ye'll sind Packy to what th' Germans call a Kindygartin, an' 'tis a good thing fr Germany, because all a German knows is what some wan tells him, an' his grajation papers is a certy-ficate that he don't need to think anny more. But we've inthrajooced it into this counthry, an' whin I was down seein' if I cud injooce Rafferry, th' Janitor iv th' Isaac Muggs Grammar School, fr to vote fr Riordan—an' he's goin' to—I dhropped in on

Cassidy's daughter, Mary Ellen, an' see her kindygartnin'. Th' childher was settin' ar-round on th' flure an' some was moldin' dachshunds out iv mud an' wipin' their hands on their hair, an' some was carvin' figures iv a goat out iv paste-board an' some was singin' an' some was sleepin' an' a few was dancin' an' wan la-ad was pullin' another la-ad's hair. 'Why don't ye take th' coal shovel to that little barbaryan, Mary Ellen?' says I. 'We don't believe in corporeal punishment,' says she. 'School shud be made pleasant fr th' childher,' she says. 'Th' child who's hair is bein' pulled is larnin' patience,' she says, 'an' th' child that's pullin' th' hair is discovrin' th' footility iv human indeavor,' says she. 'Well, oh, well,' says I, 'times has changed since I was a boy,' I says. 'Put thim through their exercises,' says I. 'Tommy,' says I, 'spell cat,' I says. 'Go to th' divvle,' says th' cheerub. 'Very smartly answered,' says Mary Ellen. 'Ye shud not ask thim to spell,' she says. 'They don't larn that till they get to colledge,' she says, 'an'' she says, 'sometimes not even thin,' she says. 'An' what do they larn?' says I. 'Rompin',' she says, 'an' dancin',' she says, 'an' indepindance iv speech, an' beauty songs, an' sweet thoughts, an' how to make home home-like,' she says. 'Well,' says I, 'I didn't take anny iv thim things at colledge, so ye needn't unblanket thim,' I says. 'I won't put thim through anny exercise today,' I says. 'But whisper, Mary Ellen,' says I, 'Don't ye niver feel like bastin' th' seeraphims?' 'Th' teachin's iv Freebull and Pitzotly is conthrary to that,' she says. 'But I'm goin' to be marrid an' lave th' school on Choosdah, th' twinty-sicond iv Janooary,' she says, 'an' on Mondah, th' twinty-first, I'm goin' to ask a few iv th' little darlin's to th' house an',' she says, 'stew thim over a slow fire,' she says. Mary Ellen is not a German, Hinnissy."

"Well, afther they have larned in school what they ar-re licked fr larnin' in th' back yard—that is squashin' mud with their hands—they're conducted up through a channel iv free an' beautiful thought till they're r-ready fr colledge. Mamma packs a few doylies an' tidies into son's bag, an' some silver to be used in case iv throuble with th' landlord, an' th' la-ad throts off to th' siminary. If he's not sthrong enough to look fr high honors as a middle weight pugilist he goes into th' thought departmint. Th' prisidint takes him into a Turkish room, gives him a cigareet an' says: 'Me dear boy, what special branch iv larnin' wud ye like to have studied fr ye be our compitint profissors? We have a chair iv Beauty an' wan iv Puns an' wan iv Pothry on th' Changin' Hues iv the Settin' Sun, an' wan on Platonic Love, an' wan on Nonsense Rhymes, an' wan on Sweet Thoughts, an' wan on How Green Grows th' Grass, an' wan on' th' Relation iv Ice to th' Greek Idee iv God,' he says. 'This is all ye'll need to equip ye fr th' perfect life, onless,' he says, 'ye intind bein' a dintist, in which case,' he says, 'we won't think much iv ye, but we have a good school where ye can larn that disgraceful thrade,' he says. An' th' la-ad makes his choice, an' ivry mornin' whin he's up in time he takes a whiff iv hasheesh an' goes off to hear Profissor Maryanna tell him that 'if th' dates iv human knowledge must be rejicted as subjictive, how much more must they be subjicted as rejictive if, as I think, we keep our thoughts fixed upon th' inanity iv th' finite in comparison with th' onthinkable truth with th' ondivided an' onimaginable reality. Boys ar-re ye with me?'"

"That's at wan colledge-Th' Colledge iv Speechless Thought. Thin there's th' Colledge iv Thoughtless Speech, where th' la-ad is larned that th' best thing that can happen to annywan is to be prisident iv a railroad consolidation. Th' head iv this colledge believes in thrainin' young men f'r th' civic ideel, Father Kelly tells me. Th' on'y thrainin' I know f'r th' civic ideel is to have an alarm clock in ye'er room on iliction day. He believes 'young men shud be equipped with Courage, Discipline, an' Loftiness iv Purpose;' so I suppose Packy, if he wint there, wud listen to lectures fr'm th' Profissor iv Courage an' Erasmus H. Noddle, Doctor iv Loftiness iv Purpose. I loft, ye loft, he lofts. I've always felt we needed some wan to teach our young th' Courage they can't get walkin' home in th' dark, an' th' loftiness iv purpose that doesn't start with bein' hungry an' lookin' f'r wurruk. An' in th' colledge where these studies are taught, its undhershtud that even betther thin gettin' th' civic ideel is bein' head iv a thrust. Th' on'y trouble with th' coorse is that whin Packy comes out loaded with loftiness iv purpose, all th' lofts is full iv men that had to figure it out on th' farm."

"I don't undherstand a wurrud iv what ye're sayin'," said Mr. Hennesy.

"No more do I," said Mr. Dooley. "But I believe 'tis as Father Kelly says: 'Childher shudden't be sint to school to larn, but to larn how to larn. I don't care what ye larn thim so long as 'tis onpleasant to thim.' 'Tis thrainin' they need, Hinnissy. That's all. I niver cud make use iv what I larned in colledge about thrigojoomethry an'—an'—grammar an' th' welts I got on th' skull fr'm the schoolmasther's cane I have nivver been able to turn to anny account in th' business, but 'twas th' bein' there and havin' to get things to heart without askin' th' meanin' iv thim an' goin' to school cold an' comin' home hungry, that made th' man iv me ye see befure ye."

"That's why th' good woman's throubled about Packy," said Hennessy.

"Go home," said Mr. Dooley.

"L'AIGLON"

"Hogan's been tellin' me iv a new play he r-read th' other day," said Mr. Dooley. "'Tis be th' same la-ad that wrote th' piece they played down in th' Christyan Brothers' school last year about the man with th' big nose, that wud dhraw a soord or a pome on e'er a man alive. This wan is called 'The Little Eagle,' an' 'tis about th' son iv Napolyon th' Impror iv th' Fr-rinch, th' first wan, not th' wan I had th' fight about in Schwartzmeister's in eighteen hundhred an' siventy. Bad cess to that man, he was no good. I often wondher why I shtud up fr him whin he had hardly wan frind in th' counthry. But I did, an' ye might say I'm a vethran iv th' Napolyonic Wars. I am so.

"But th' first Napolyon was a diff'rent man, an' whin he died he left a son that th' coorts tur-rned over to th' custody iv his mother, th' ol' man bein' on th' island—th' same place where Gin'ral Crownjoy is now. Tis about this la-ad th' play's written. He don't look to be much account havin' a hackin' cough all through the piece, but down undherneath he wants to be impror iv th' Fr-rinch like his father befure him, d'ye mind, on'y he don't dare to go out fr it fr fear iv catchin' a bad cold on his chist. Th' Austhreeches that has charge iv him don't like th' idee iv havin' him know what kind iv man his father was. Whin he asks: 'Where's pah?' They say: 'He died in jail.' 'What happened in 1805?' says th' boy. 'In 1805,' says th' Austhreeches, 'th' bar-rn blew down.' 'In 1806?' says th' boy. 'In 1806 th' chimney smoked.' 'Not so,' says th' prince. 'In 1806 me father crossed th' Rhine an' up,' he says, 'th' ar-rmed camps he marched to Augaspiel, to Lieberneck, to Donnervet. He changed his boots at Mikelstraus an' down th' eagle swooped on Marcobrun,' he says. 'Me gran'dad fled as flees th' hen befure th' hawk, but dad stayed not till gran'pa, treed, besought fr peace. That's what me father done unto me gran'dad in eighteen six.' At this p'int he coughs but ye sees he knew what was goin' on, bein' taught in secret be a lady iv th' stage fr'm whom manny a la-ad cud larn th' truth about his father.

"Still he can't be persuaded fr to apply fr th' vacant improrship on account iv his lungs, till wan day a tailor shows up to measure him fr some clothes. Th' tailor d'ye mind is a rivolutionist in disguise, an' has come down fr'm Paris fr to injooce th' young man to take th' vacancy. 'Fourteen, six, thirty-three. How'll ye have th' pants made, Impror?' says th' tailor. 'Wan or two hip pockets?' says he.

"'Two hips,' says young Napolyon. 'What do ye mean be that?'" he says.

"'Thirty-eight, siventeen, two sides, wan watch, buckle behind. All Paris awaits ye, sire.'"

"'Make th' sleeves a little longer thin this,' says th' boy. 'An' fill out th' shouldhers. What proof have I?'"

"'Wan or two inside pockets?' says th' tailor. 'Two insides. Hankerchief pocket? Wan hankerchief. Th' pants is warn much fuller this year. Make that twinty-eight instid iv twinty-siven,' he says. 'Paris shrieks f'r ye,' he says.

"'Proof,' says th' la-ad.

"'They've named a perfume afther ye, a shirt waist, a paper collar, a five cint seegar, a lot iv childer. Nay more, a breakfast dish christened f'r ye is on ivry lip. Will I forward th' soot collect?' he says.

"'No, sind th' bill to me mother,' says th' boy. 'An' meet me in th' park at tin,' he says.

"So 'tis planned to seize th' throne, but it comes to nawthin'."

"Why's that?" asked Mr. Hennessy.

"F'r th' same reason that the Irish rivolution failed, th' polis stopped it. Th' conspirators met in th' park an' were nailed be a park polisman. They didn't run in th' boy, but left him alone in th' place which was where his father wanst fought a battle. As he shtands there coughin' he begins to hear voices iv soops that followed th' ol' Impror. 'Comrade' says wan. 'Give me ye'er hand.' 'I can't,' says another. 'I haven't wan left.' 'Where's me leg?' 'Sarch me.' 'I've lost me voice.' 'Me mind is shot away.' 'Reach me some wather.' 'Pass th' can.' 'A horse is settin' on me chest.' 'What's that? They'se a batthry iv artillery on me.' 'I've broke something. What is it?' 'I cannot move me leg.' 'Curses on the Cavalry.' 'Have ye got th' time?' 'Oh me knee, how it aches me.' 'Ha ha. Ha ha. Ha ha. Ha ha.' 'Veev, th' Impror.' 'Right about face, shouldher ar-rms, right shouldher shift arms. March.' A harsh, metallic voice in the distance: 'Gin-rals, leftnant Gin'rals, officers, sooz-officers, an' men—.' 'Tis th' boy's father. Th' boy pulls out his soord an' says he: 'Come on, let's fight. Play away there band. Blow fife and banners wave. Lave me at thim. Come on, come on!' an' he rushes out an' makes a stab at an Austhreech regimint that's come up to be dhrilled. Thin he undherstands 'twas all a dhream with him an' he raysumes his ol' job. In th' next act he dies."

"That's a good act," said Mr. Hennessy.

"'Tis fine. In Austhree where this happened whin a man dies ivrybody comes in to see him. Ye meet a frind on th' sthreet an' he says: 'Come on over an see Harrigan jump off.' So whin th' la-ad is r-ready f'r to go out ivry body gathers in his room. 'Tis a fash'nable ivint, like th' Horse Show. Among those prisint is his mother. She's a frivolous ol' loon, this Marie Louisa, that was Napolyon's sicond wife, though between you an' me, Father Kelly has niver reconized her as such, th' Impror havin' a wife livin' that was as tough as they make thim. But annyhow she was there. She hadn't done much f'r her son, but she come to see him off with siv'ral ladies that loved him an' others. Bein' a busy an' fashn'able woman she cudden't raymimber his name. At times she called him 'Frank' an' thin 'Fronzwah' an' 'Fritz' an' 'Ferdynand'—'twas a name beginnin' with 'f' she knew that—but he f'rgive her an' ast somewan to r-read to him. 'What shall it be?' says a gin'ral. 'R-read about th' time I was christened,' says th' boy. An' th' gin'ral r-reads: 'At iliven o'clock at th' church iv Nothre Dame in th' prisince iv th' followin' princes—,' 'Cut out th' princes,' says th' la-ad. 'An' kings—' 'F'rget th' kings,' says th' lad. 'Th' son iv th' Impror—' 'He's dead,' says th' doctor. 'Put on his white soot,' says th' Main Thing among th' Austhreeches that was again him fr'm th' beginnin'. An' there ye ar-re."

"Is that all?" asked Mr. Hennessy.

"That's all," said Mr. Dooley.

"He died?"

"He did."

"But he was sthrong r-right up to th' end."

"He was that. None sthronger."

"An' what?" asked Mr. Hennessy, "did they do with th' soot iv clothes he ordhered fr'm th' tailor?"

www.ingramcontent.com/pod-product-compliance
Lightning Source LLC
Chambersburg PA
CBHW081201020426
42333CB00020B/2587